FLORIDA

IN THE
SPANISH-
AMERICAN WAR

FLORIDA

—— IN THE ——
SPANISH-
AMERICAN WAR

JOE KNETSCH & NICK WYNNE

Charleston   London

THE
History
PRESS

Published by The History Press
Charleston, SC 29403
www.historypress.net

Cover image: The *Sinking of the Maine, 1898*. Courtesy of Arva Parks McCabe.

First published 2011

Manufactured in the United States

ISBN 978.1.60949.088.1

Library of Congress Cataloging-in-Publication Data

Knetsch, Joe.
Florida in the Spanish-American War / Joe Knetsch and Nick Wynne.
p. cm.
Includes bibliographical references.
ISBN 978-1-60949-088-1
1. Spanish-American War, 1898--Florida. 2. Florida--History,
Military--19th century. I. Wynne, Nick. II. Title.
E726.F6K64 2011
975.9'04--dc22
2010049063

For Linda Knetsch

and

Debra and Lisa Wynne

CONTENTS

Acknowledgements

Authors do not write books in isolation. Most books are the result of collaboration between the writers and scores of other people who provide information, point to new sources and offer critical suggestions. This book is certainly the result of collaborations that extend over many years. To all of those who helped us, we offer our sincere thanks.

Susan Carter and the staff at the Henry B. Plant Museum and Archives were very helpful. So, too, were Ross Lamoreaux and Jennifer Diehl at the Tampa Bay History Center. The same could be said for Alexander Buell and Teen Peterson at the Amelia Island Museum of History. Dr. James Cusick at the University of Florida's P.K. Yonge Library contributed photographs and advice—thank you, Jim. Jennifer Amy, Barbara West, George L. Harrell and Robert Gross at the Florida Historical Society made collections available and gave encouragement. They are good folks. Debi Murray at the Historical Society of Palm Beach County also provided much-appreciated photographs and information. The assistance of the staff of the State Library of Florida—especially Linda Pulliam, Cindy Chillingsworth, Deborah Mekeel and Laura Baas and their colleagues in the State Archives of Florida—has been invaluable. Arva Parks McCabe, a Miami historian, graciously allowed us to use photographs from her collection.

The following people also assisted us in obtaining information or acted as sounding boards to some of our ideas: Ed Keuchel, Bill Adams, Cecile Sastre, Cleve Powell, Tom Hambright, Pamela Gibson, Pamela Vojnovski, Rodney Dillon, Barbara Poleo, Tom Knowles, Joan Langley, Sam Watson, Alan Aimone, Nick Reynolds, Harold Raugh, Nick Hollar, Fred Holzbaur, Heidi Weber, Martin Gordon, Celeste and Clinch Kavanaugh, John and Mary Lou

Missall, Charles Herner, Brian Rucker, Sarah Nell Gran, Larry Wiggins, Kevin Hooper, Claude Kennison, Consuelo Stebbins, Bill Crawford, Rodney Kite-Powell, Liz Dunham, Paul Camp, Jerry Casale, Bob Gross, Charlie Corbett, Jody Miller, Jorge Alonzo and Roger Cunningham. Last, but surely not least, we need to thank Debra Wynne, who, while serving as the archivist for the Florida Historical Society's Library of Florida History, provided much information and support.

Much of the information that appears in this book is the result of years of research and analysis. Some of the information challenges the prevailing interpretations of America's involvement in the Spanish-American War, and portions of the material have been presented in academic papers at conferences and historical society meetings in order to provoke discussions and to elicit the opinions of other professional historians. With the vast amounts of previously unknown or unused sources/resources that are readily available, the time has come to reexamine the causes, costs and results of the war.

INTRODUCTION

*The pacifist is as surely a traitor to his country and to humanity as is the
most brutal wrongdoer.*
—Theodore Roosevelt

Florida has always had a strong connection with Spain and Cuba. Spanish authorities—both church and state—governed the peninsula from Havana when Florida was a small, but very important, colony of the Spanish Empire. Its strategic location allowed Spain to control the Florida Straights, the gateway to Central and South America, and to protect its treasure galleons using the Gulf Stream to carry the plunder of the Americas to Spain. By the early 1700s, Spain considered Florida so important to its efforts to block French and English colonization of North America that it continued to commit men and money to maintain the small garrisons that manned Pensacola and St. Augustine, even though it got little in return. Unlike most of Spain's colonial possessions, the Florida peninsula contributed almost nothing to the Spanish treasury. Still, its value as a military outpost forced Spain to continue occupation of Florida.

Even as the Spanish Empire began to shrink, Florida and Cuba remained important possessions. In 1819, Spain agreed to cede Florida to the United States in exchange for forgiveness of $5 million in debts. American annexation did not end Spanish influence on the peninsula, nor did it sever relations between Americans and Cubans. Throughout the nineteenth century, a constant flow of cattle and agricultural produce moved between the island and the peninsula. During the Civil War, both Confederate and Union forces used Cuban ports to replenish their ships, as an intelligence center and as a transit point for shipping.

When the Civil War ended in 1865, Americans set out to pacify the western Indians and to open the vast expanses between St. Louis and San Francisco to settlement. The massive Federal army of the war years was reduced to a small force of twenty-five thousand men, while the American navy, which had been strong enough to blockade much of the Atlantic coast, was allowed to shrink. Although the industrial might of the United States was unequaled by any other country, very few resources were dedicated to improving and upgrading the military forces of the nation. Supplies left over from the Civil War filled huge warehouses and continued to be the primary supply sources for the army and navy. Exhausted and scarred by the horrors of the Civil War, few military leaders and fewer civilians saw the need to invest in upgrading the nation's forces.

By 1885, the western territories were largely pacified. Railroads spanned the continent, bringing a civilized veneer to faraway towns and villages. Immigrants from Europe poured into the United States, providing a growing labor force for industries and taking advantage of the cheap land available for settlement. Development of America's natural resources and the expansion of factories to supply the demands of its burgeoning population focused the attention of the nation internally.

While Americans were preoccupied with their development, other countries were concerned about gaining a foothold as colonial powers. Recently united Germany and Italy looked to Africa as a good place to acquire colonies at a cheap price. In the Far East, Japan, which had been opened to the rest of the world in the 1850s, embraced the processes of industrial development, and Japanese military leaders, aware of the superiority of western arms, rushed to equip their forces with the latest technological developments in land and sea warfare. The aggressiveness of these newer nations provoked tensions and minor confrontations with the older colonial powers—Great Britain, Spain and France—destabilizing the world situation.

Protected by its long coasts, the United States continued to develop its internal empire, only occasionally stirring to wave the flag of the uncertain Monroe Doctrine when events in the Americas threatened its perceived interests. There were thinkers in the American political and military establishments who raised concerns about the failure of the United States to field an army and navy that matched those of other countries in size and effectiveness. There were other Americans who envied the colonial powers and their seizure of large and wealthy colonies in Africa and the Far East, while a coterie of younger souls, raised on stories of the valor and gallantry of soldiers in the Civil War, urged the United States to take a more active role in world affairs, even if it meant fighting small wars.

As new colonies were acquired by emerging nations, Spain, possessor of the oldest empire, found itself fighting wars to prevent its colonies from breaking away. Over the course of the nineteenth century, the cost of fighting wars of independence, particularly in Central and South America, had depleted the Spanish treasury. Yet Spain could not surrender its colonies without fighting. To do so would mark it as a weak, second-rate power, and all of its colonial possessions would become fair game for other, stronger powers or would fall like dominoes to indigenous revolutionaries. Spain faced a conundrum—to fight would further weaken its economy, but not fighting would ensure the hasty loss of its empire.

In the 1890s, Spain faced another dilemma. Insurgents in Cuba again took to the field against Spanish authorities. This was only one of several revolutions against Spanish rule of that island that had been fought since the mid-1800s. By pursuing a policy of brutal suppression, Spain had managed to retain nominal control of the island, but brutality as a policy of suppression was a double-edged sword. While the use of overwhelming force and brutality might temporarily end a rebellion, such actions left a residue of hatred that fueled another outbreak later. Such policies also brought the condemnation of other nations, especially at the end of the century when newspapers around the world sent reporters to cover the conflicts.

As Spanish resources dwindled, Cuban revolutionaries were able to gain support from citizens of the United States, Cuban exiles and other revolutionary groups in Latin America. Men, equipment and money, brought to Cuba by filibustering expeditions from Florida ports, made it difficult for Spain to bring the revolution to an end.

The sinking of the American battleship *Maine*, sent to Cuba to show the flag and to provide protection for American citizens and business interests, changed the Cuban conflict from revolution to war. American newspapers, politicians and militarists blamed Spain for the sinking and demanded that President William McKinley, a cautious man, ask Congress for a declaration of war. Spain desperately tried to defuse the situation, but on April 25, 1898, Congress approved a declaration of war, retroactive to April 22.

John Hay, the American ambassador to Great Britain, declared it to be "a splendid little war" from start to finish, while William Randolph Hearst, publisher of the *San Francisco Examiner* and the *New York Journal*, claimed personal ownership of the war and referred to it as the "*Journal's* war." Theodore Roosevelt, always ready to comment on current events, said simply, "It isn't much of a war, but, hell, it's the only war we've got." It was the worldwide conflict between an old colonial power—Spain—and the emerging world

Many Americans felt that war with a common enemy—Spain—for Cuban freedom (personified in the center of this photograph) would heal any remaining wounds from the Civil War. The Spanish-American War is sometimes referred to as the "War of National Reunification." *Courtesy of the Florida Historical Society.*

power, the United States. Other editors played up the angle that war with Spain was a surefire way to reunite the northern and southern states and to erase any lingering hard feelings over the Civil War.

War, when it came, seemed to offer something positive to almost all Americans. The America that emerged from the war would be radically different from the nation that entered the war.

1

FLORIDA IN THE LATE
NINETEENTH CENTURY

The greatest of all Florida's resources is the fertility of its agricultural lands.
Every intelligent investor in Florida property realizes that the value of his
investment is in a large measure based upon the development of the State's
agricultural resources.
—Florida in the Making, *1926*

The economy of Florida in the years after Reconstruction was in the doldrums, and Floridians experienced economic woes unlike any they had faced before. The agricultural labor market was no longer slave based, and new relationships between former masters and slaves had to be formed. The government was deeply in debt because of the war, while property values plummeted to new lows. The trustees of the Internal Improvement Fund—an arm of the government that had been assigned the task of ensuring that railroads, a single transportation canal and other improvements would be built and paid for with the sale of public lands—were hamstrung to pump money into the economy because of the huge debts created by the state government to pay for Florida's participation in the Civil War. The failure of the Confederate States of America to gain independence left the state with a treasury filled with worthless Confederate money, obligations to pay for military equipment it had purchased during the war, a citizenry that was broke and a credit rating that made any loans, backed by bonds, impossible to secure.

By 1880, the state's debt neared $1 million, an almost unheard-of sum for that day and age, and until it could improve its credit rating enough to persuade investors to commit their money to buy Florida bonds, the Sunshine State was forced to limp along near bankruptcy. Although the state owned vast acreages of public land, this asset could not be converted into cash, and as a result, no new improvements to the state's transportation system could be made. With the existing transportation system in shambles, farmers were unable to market their crops of tobacco, citrus and cotton to national and world markets. Floridians, particularly those in the interior of the state, struggled to survive. Until the labor situation was resolved and new relationships forged between landowners and laborers, little hope existed for creating a vibrant and profitable economy. Even when some progress was made at the local level, the state's massive debt limited its ability to provide much-needed assistance in devising ways to get crops to market. Florida was an economic backwater, hampered by its size and the poverty of its people and government, and was seemingly destined to remain so.

When viewed from a national perspective, Florida was at a competive disadvantage compared to the rising states and territories of the American West. The 1870s and 1880s were years of tremendous investments in advertising American lands on the frontiers of the West. The large land grant railroads, aided by generous grants, subsidies and exemptions from taxation in many areas, were able to invest in sending brochures, agents and other materials back east or to Europe, where very imaginative campaigns were being launched to attract settlers. Many of these railroads offered cheap land near the railroads, and many offered attractive payment plans to get future inhabitants interested in migrating to the frontiers.

As migration often follows parallels of latitude, the northern areas held an edge in attracting prospective immigrants. Florida, being farther south and nearly semitropical, did not appear attractive enough to settlers from northern Europe, particularly Scandanavia, even though Henry Sanford was able to attract some to the Florida wilderness near Lake Monroe. Sanford's brave quest yielded very little when compared to the efforts of Minnesota, Wisconsin, the Dakotas and the lands in the upper Red River Valley of the North. There were so few operating railroads in Florida, and most of the interior was undeveloped because of the lack of roads, that, coupled with the absence of plentiful deep-water ports, it was extremely difficult to attract new settlers to the Sunshine State. While the state legislature did try, on more than one occasion, to develop an immigration bureau and send representatives to Europe, the actual funding of these efforts was too small to effect any meaningful change.

Flordia's reputation as the home of mosquitoes, snakes and alligators did not enhance the desirability of the state as a destination for final settlement. The collective memory of many northerners was cluttered with images of Florida as a wilderness, inhabited by "savage" Seminoles and their allies. Three

Tourists enjoyed observing Florida's flora and fauna aboard the small steamships that cruised its inland waterways. This postcard depicted a pleasure boat cruising on the Ocklawaha River. *Courtesy of the Ada E. Parrish Postcard Collection.*

pre-1860 wars with this group of Indians certainly inhibited the development of the state greatly, and the reports home by officers and troops serving in Florida were none too flattering. These images remained after the Civil War and served to create negative feelings against possible in-migration by other Americans to the Sunshine State. Slogging through the infamous swamps of southern Florida or along the the sharp-rocked coasts did not sound enticing to many potential settlers. True, northern Florida mirrored southern Georgia in climate and soil, and it was possible to grow creditable amounts of cotton, sugar and some tobacco, but the perception of Florida as an uninviting and wild frontier—a residual effect of the three wars with the Seminoles— dampened the desire of outsiders to come to Florida. Even with the Armed Occupation Act of 1842, the Graduation Act, the Homestead Act and other enticements, few actually migrated to the Sunshine State. By 1880, the state had only 269,500 total population. But that was about to change.

The primary problem for the state was the lack of transportation, which stemmed from a shortage of state funding and a federal injunction against the state, secured by Francis Vose and other investors for money due them on the earlier government-backed railroad bonds, which prevented Florida's

Much of Florida's economy in the post–Civil War years rested on the exploitation of its timber and naval stores. *Courtesy of the Florida Historical Society.*

government from finding new sources of money to fund development. In 1881, with the advent of the first administration of Governor William Bloxham, the situation changed dramatically when the governor and other leaders persuaded the Philadelphia investor Hamilton Disston to pay off the $1 million debt in return for four million acres of swamp and overflowed lands. Disston, who was already at work draining a portion of the upper Kissimmee River Valley, was eager to drain the lands and make them productive. He quickly found other investors to share his dream, and the Disston Land Company and a large number of subsidiary firms were created to sell and develop these lands. The deal freed the Florida government from its burdensome debt and allowed the state to use the remaining swamplands as enticements for railroad builders and other types of investors.

It is not coincidence that Henry Flagler, Henry Plant, William Chipley and others all began massive railroad construction and riverboat projects in the 1880s. Their success in creating a far-reaching transportation infrastucture opened up the state for further development and immigration. Indeed, railroads soon began flooding Europe and the northern states with brochures, pamphlets and other materials touting the state's wonderful resources, climate

In the late nineteenth century, Florida was a state that depended on agriculture and cattle ranching, with a few tourists in St. Augustine and along the coasts. In 1894, it was the nation's chief producer of pineapples. *Courtesy of the Ada E. Parrish Postcard Collection.*

and new rail system, since these companies knew that they needed to sell the land they had secured as subsidies in order to make a profit. These same brochures, pamphlets and other materials also introduced the new crop that was to make everyone's fortunes: citrus. The 1880s and 1890s saw the state almost double in population, and "orange gold" was the main attraction. The new transportation network that evolved from the work of the railroad builders made it easier and less expensive for immigrants to choose to come to Florida and try their hands at growing the profitable citrus crops.

The railroads, besides adding their financial resources to the push for immigration, also spurred a number of other industries, including truck farming, tie cutting, timber exports and construction. In a minor irony of the day, Florida attracted a number of African American workers and was one of only two southern states (the other was Texas) that showed a growth in this segment of the population from the early 1880s until 1900. In addition, investors seeking other uses for their landholdings quickly discovered and exploited the vast phosphate deposits in the "Bone Valley," which extended from near the city of Dunnellon through the entire valley of the southern Withlacoochee River, through Polk and Hillsborough Counties and along the

Peace River Valley almost to Charlotte Harbor. The growth of the phosphate industry; the harvesting of yellow pine, cypress and cedar; and the construction of railroads and drainage canals were all labor-intensive enterprises that depended on large numbers of menial workers, black and white.

Labor recruiters brought large numbers of workers to Florida in the two decades prior to the outbreak of the Spanish-American War. These industries also brought large amounts of outside investments from Europe and the northern states, undeterred by the vagaries of international and national markets. Overproduction of citrus, for example, steadily dampened the profitability of that industry and produced wild swings in the price per box of Florida citrus. The War of the Pacific (often called the "Great Guano War"), fought over the right to extract vast quantities of bird droppings for use as fertilizer, had its impact on the production of and demand for Florida phosphate. Like cotton and tobacco farmers, citrus farmers and mining companies soon found themselves operating in unstable markets and were unable to rely on steady prices from year to year. Overall, however, the economy of Florida flourished in the years following the Disston Purchase.

The decade of the 1890s was one of the most volatile in the history of Florida. The prosperity ushered in by the phosphate, lumber and citrus industries brought great wealth into the state. Expectations were high among the newcomers and old-timers alike. Florida had never experienced growth of such magnitude and volume, and many expected this to last longer than it could logically sustain itself. A sense of optimism replaced the pessimism of the Reconstruction era, and it seemed that the Sunshine State had at last embarked on a course to permanent prosperity, but that optimism would soon be challenged.

Like the rest of the nation, Florida was not ready for the sharp and severe Depression of 1893–94. The inflated values of real estate, the overextension of credit and the uncertainty of the currency and instability in the banking systems created problems everywhere. Unemployment in the industrial North and quickly deflated prices for southern and western agricultural products led to the rise of extremist political parties seeking to use the economic crisis to gain control of the federal government and statehouses across the nation. In particular, the growing Populist movement, seeking to unite farmers, laborers, African Americans and poor whites, attacked the established Democratic and Republican parties as "tools of the rich." Democrat Grover Cleveland was the president unlucky enough to be in office when the depression began, and his "hard-money" stance made him the darling of the established business interests but also made him an anathema to the Populists and to many in the

President Grover Cleveland was the only American president to serve two terms as chief executive separated by four years. *Courtesy of the Florida Historical Society.*

Democratic party, who saw their rare postwar chance at governance (spoils) on the wane again.

Orders for Florida products fell quickly, and prices fell below the costs of production, severely reducing the income of farmers and citrus growers and restricting their access to credit. Many blamed the railroads and their alleged high rates for their problems, others looked to the politicians as the fall guys and still others looked to the financial community, with its call for keeping the United States on the gold standard, for culprits. William Jennings Bryan, a dynamic orator from Nebraska, moved to the center of the nation's political scene with his empassioned speeches for silver to become a basis for the nation's currency along with gold at a ratio of sixteen to one. The inclusion of silver to back the currency would make more money available, end the credit crunch and invigorate the nation's marketplaces. The cry of "Free Silver!" would dominate the presidential election of 1896 when Bryan became the Democratic nominee.

With their expectations shattered by forces beyond their control, Floridians were already in foul moods when the weather turned against them. Following quickly on the heels of the Depression of 1893–94 came the catastrophic freezes of late 1894–95. Thousands of Floridians had invested in family-sized citrus groves, hoping to cash in on the new growth industry of the day. The freezes of this tragic season were to crush those dreams. Within a span of less than three months, beginning on December 27, 1894, the citrus crop of Florida was almost totally wiped out, and the fortunes of those banking on the expected crop were erased with it. Thousands attempted to sell their lands but, finding few takers, just abandoned their Florida hopes and returned to wherever they had called home prior to their move southward. Even menial jobs requiring little training or investment, like tie cutting or picking citrus, were not available. Competition for the remaining jobs was stiff and would soon turn violent.

About the only industry that avoided much of these difficult times was the cattle industry, which still had its traditional Cuban market and a suprisingly steady domestic market for its products. But cow hunting required skill and endurance to face the frontier conditions of Florida's palmetto and scrub pine range, and as the market for the cattle industry remained relatively stable at this time, there was not a large increase in demand for cow hunters, as Florida cowboys are called. Hence there was no job growth worthy of the name in this industry either.

With hopes dashed by the freezes, little growth in the economy and Florida's traditionally low wage scale, the unemployed grew increasingly unhappy and more militant. Some political observers feared that a workers' revolution would evolve out of the desperate economic conditions faced by the lower classes. It was a concern that would emerge again and again over the next several decades, fueling Theodore Roosevelt's Square Deal reforms and Franklin Delano Roosevelt's New Deal policies.

2

CUBANS, FLORIDA AND CUBA LIBRE

*Let us sing today an anthem to life before their
well remembered graves.
Yesterday I heard it, rising from the earth itself
as I crossed the dreary afternoon on my way
to this faithful town...
Amidst the shredded clouds, a pine tree defied the storm
and thrust the stately trunk upwards.
Suddenly, the sun broke through a forest clearing,
and there, by a swift flash of light I saw, rising from the
yellowed grass amidst the blackened trunks of the fallen pines,
the joyful shoots of the new pines.
That is what we are: new pines!
—José Martí, November 27, 1891*

Cuban migration into the United States had centered on Florida during the years after the Ten Years' War (1868–78). The immediate center of trade and migration revolved around the city of Key West, where a number of cigar makers located their new plants. At the time, Key West was the largest city in Florida and had a long history of trade with Cuba and other Spanish possessions. The first cigar plant in Key West was established in 1831 by William H. Wall and operated until a fire destroyed it in 1859. Employing fifty workers in the manufacturing of cigars, it was one of the largest private employers in the city. This was followed soon thereafter by the Estava & Williams firm, which began operations in 1837 and shipped its products directly to New York. The Arnau brothers also began making and shipping

☆ CLEAR HAVANA
☆ EXTREMELY MILD

Straights

Cubans made up the majority of cigar workers in Key West, Ocala, Jacksonville and Tampa. In Tampa, two major centers of cigar production, Ybor City and West Tampa, produced more cigars than the other cities combined. *Courtesy of the Florida Historical Society.*

cigars from Key West in 1838, and others soon followed their example. The largest migration of Cubans to Key West came in the wake of the Ten Years' War when most of the better-known cigar makers made their way to Key West and, later, to Tampa.

By the 1870s, Seidenberg & Company, the Hirsch Company, the Ruy Lopez Company and the "El Principe de Gales" of Vincente Martinez Ybor were in full operation and shipping their now famous cigars to New York and other world markets. Labor problems, especially in the Seidenberg establishment, and the great fire of 1886 convinced some of the manufacturers that another location might be desirable, and the little town of Tampa, numbering only 720 residents in 1880, sent a committee to Key West to convince the owners of the potential of that town. Ybor and others soon found the location to their liking and began moving operations to Tampa in the late 1880s. This movement

Many Americans embraced the cause of Cuba Libre as justification for entering a war with Spain. Spain had fought Cuban guerillas since the late 1860s, so the idea was not a new one. *Courtesy of the Henry B. Plant Museum Archives, Tampa.*

not only brought some economic development and population to Tampa, but also, within the working class of cigar makers, it carried with it the spirit of Cuban liberty. Many of the workers who came to Florida from Cuba at this time came to continue the fight for Cuba Libre and to escape the near anarchy that was threatening to destroy that country. The turmoil in Cuba and the revolutionary fervor of many who came to Florida made the Sunshine State a ripe ground for recruitment and funding of future revolutionary ventures.

The importance of the Cuban migration to Florida cannot be overstated. After the founding of the modern cigar manufacturing plants in Key West, the Cuban population began to exercise its newfound political rights. The first of the newspapers dedicated to exercising the right to a free press was *El Republicano*, which was owned by Juan M. Reyes and began operating in 1870. Although many other newspapers were published for Cubans in Key

José Martí, a Cuban leader for independence, was a frequent visitor to Fernandina, Tampa and Key West. The cigar workers in these small cities contributed money for the cause of Cuban freedom. José Martí was killed in battle against Spanish troops at the Battle of Dos Ríos, on May 19, 1895. *Courtesy of the Tampa Bay History Center.*

West, the most important appears to have been J.D. Poyo's *El Yara*. Poyo was the major voice for the Cuba Libre movement in Key West and was a close correspondent with the revolutionary leader José Martí. Poyo not only backed the revolutionary movement but also promoted Cuban participation in Florida politics.

The Cuban population of Key West, according to Jefferson Browne, was not partisan in its politics but voted for both Democrats and Republicans in local elections. As the "swing vote" in many such elections, Cubans were able to send Morua P. Delgado, Dr. Manuel R. Moreno and J.G. Pompez to the state legislature and elected Carlos de Cespedes (the son of a leading revolutionary of the Ten Years' War) as mayor of Key West in 1876. One of the more notable Cubans who took part in the American system was Fernando Figueredo, who was elected to the Florida legislature in 1884 and who later became superintendent of public instruction for Monroe County.

Among the leaders of the revolutionary organizations in Key West were Figueredo and Poyo.

The migration of Cubans to Tampa and its surroundings came in the early 1880s and allegedly stemmed from a search for usable guava trees by food exporter Gavino Guteirrez. Guteirrez had been told of Tampa's plentiful wild guava trees, and this interested him in establishing a guava jelly manufacturing concern. Although there were not enough trees to make the proposition work, he was impressed enough with the Tampa area that he spread the word of its worth to friends in Key West, principle among whom were Ybor and Ignacio Haya. Henry Bradley Plant had just completed the first rail line into Tampa at the time of their visit, and this was impressive enough to convince Ybor's partner, Eduardo Manrara, to relocate there after the fire in 1886. Manrara had an intense dislike of Key West's isolation and dependence on oceangoing traffic. He much preferred to ship his valuable cigars by rail when he had the opportunity.

Ybor and the other cigar manufacturers drove a hard bargain and even threatened to take their proposed manufacturing center to Galveston, Texas, when the city leaders failed to give them financial assistance in making the move north. The Tampa Board of Trade, realizing the importance of bringing an established industry to the city, formed the Ybor Fund Committee to raise funds needed to meet Ybor and friends' demands. In 1885, the negotiations were completed for the beginnings of Ybor City, a Tampa suburb located north of Tampa's port. By 1889, the new town was producing fifty million cigars and paying out wages amounting to over $1 million. The Ybor City Land and Development Company helped to attract workers and other industries, particularly cigar label and box makers. The company also built a rail line one and a half miles into the city of Tampa. The infusion of people and money made Tampa one of the state's leading industrial centers.

At the same time, West Tampa rose from the palmetto scrub and quickly became home to a number of cigar-manufacturing establishments. Developer Hugh C. Macfarlane acquired 120 acres of scrubland and laid out the streets of the new town. Seeking cigar manufacturers to bring their businesses to his new town of West Tampa, he offered them rent-free deals on factories he built for them. The first of these establishments came in 1892 when the Del Pino brothers accepted Macfarlane's offer and moved into a factory at the corner of today's Howard and Union Streets. The first sixty workers employed by the Del Pino brothers were mostly men from Key West who had moved with their jobs to West Tampa. Six other factories soon followed the Del Pinos, and soon West Tampa was home to more cigar factories than Ybor City. The conditions there were rather crude compared to those in Key West and the rapidly developing Ybor City, but soon the small town sported parks, broad streets and other civil amenities.

With the arrival of the O'Halloran cigar plant and the establishment of the new Armina Cigar Corporation with Macfarlane as its president, the town was soon connected to Tampa and Ybor City by a new trolley line. By 1896, forty-two cigar-manufacturing concerns had relocated or were established in West Tampa. The Monroe Cigar Company, Ceusta-Rey and others soon were putting West Tampa on the map and trading throughout the nation. The growth of the Cuban population in Florida became centered on Tampa, and by time of the Spanish-American War in 1898, fifty thousand Cuban immigrants lived within a one-hundred-mile radius of Tampa. New York and Key West, the other centers of Cuban immigration in the United States, had a combined total of only seventy-five thousand. Together, the Florida cities of Tampa, Key West, Ocala and Jacksonville were home to more immigrants from that troubled island than any other state in the nation.

Not all Spanish and Cuban immigrants to the United States were politically active or supported the idea of Cuba Libre. Many of those who came to Key West and the Tampa area were of direct Spanish descent and opposed the Cuban revolution. At one point, tensions between Cuban and Spanish cigar makers in Key West were so high that the city's leaders felt it necessary to send a committee to Havana to discuss the immigration problem with Spanish authorities and to assure them that Spaniards would receive the same protection as other United States citizens. The Tampa area, too, had a large number of Spaniards who demanded assurances of protection, and even after these assurances were given, they were not completely certain they would be honored.

When the revolution of 1895 started, hostilities between the Spanish inhabitants of Tampa and the Cuban population of the city increased. Under the leadership of Ignacio Haya, the Centro Español, with a membership of over two hundred, was built to promote a sense of unity among Spanish immigrants, who also created separate parks, churches and other social venues for their exclusive enjoyment. By 1896, tensions between ethnic groups in Ybor City were so high and the incidents of violence so frequent that Spanish residents asked the Spanish vice-consul, Pedro Solis, to submit a resolution to the City of Tampa to halt the rallies, inflammatory speeches, fundraising events and other activities being conducted by pro–Cuban independence residents. The resolution represented the wishes of some two thousand Spanish inhabitants of Tampa. Historian Joan Steffy described Ybor City as a town that "had been virtually flooded with guns awaiting shipment to Cuba,

Lieutenant General Antonio de la Caridad Maceo y Grajales (June 14, 1845–December 7, 1896) was second in command of the Cuban Army of Independence. He was a popular figure among supporters of the cause of Cuban independence. *Courtesy of the Tampa Bay History Center.*

or in the hands of future soldiers—the number of crimes involving violence increased in geometric proportions. The criminal accounts of the mid-nineties in Tampa read as if the town was itself a microcosm of the turmoil in Cuba." Any reading of the newspapers of the day would convince most people that the West was not the only wild place in America.

Ybor City and West Tampa proved to be fertile grounds for Cuban revolutionaries to plow. Virtually every well-known Cuban patriot paid a visit to the area to raise funds and to recruit new soldiers. Perhaps José Martí was best known, and he was a welcome guest at the homes of leading Cuban manufacturers, who allowed him time to make speeches to their workers. A noted poet and writer, Martí swayed supporters with a subtle mixture of passion, political rhetoric and poetry. All of Florida—from Fernandina to Key West and from Jacksonville to Ocala and Tampa—proved important sources of men, money and materiel for the Cuban cause, and Martí proved to be an excellent miner.

Florida's political problems were not limited to conflicts between the Spanish and Cubans. The 1890s in America were also violent and bloody for African Americans, and Florida was not immune to racial violence. The 1890s saw an increase in the black populations of Florida and Texas, while the rest

José Martí, pictured on the extreme right behind the small child, was the symbol of Cuban independence during the 1880s and 1890s. He is shown here with supporters during a visit to Key West. *Courtesy of the Historical Association of South Florida.*

of the South saw its black population decline. At the beginning of the decade, jobs open to blacks were mostly confined to extractive industries and farming. Florida's African American population found work opportunities in mining, timber, naval stores operations, citrus farming and warehousing. However, with the sharp and severe Panic of 1893–94, the economy began to falter, and workers in all ethnic groups found it difficult to find employment. From the largest to the smallest businesses, financial problems were a reality of daily life, and businesses were reluctant to keep large labor forces. Unemployment rates soared to new heights.

When the Reading, Northern Pacific, Union Pacific, Erie and Santa Fe Railroads all went into receivership and nearly one-fourth of all railroad capitalization was in the hands of bankruptcy courts, smaller businesses hoarded their resources and refused to expand operations. In the days before a regulated national banking system, such panics led to a decrease in the value of all currency and an increase in gold payments for goods and services from foreign sources but a decline in the purchase of American-made goods overseas. The protectionist policies of the government did little to free up money and goods for use by the average consumer. Angry unemployed workers looked for someone, almost anyone, to blame for their economic problems, and in many places, competition for jobs led to increased racial violence. Florida was just such a place.

The panic in late 1893 coincided in Florida with abundant harvests of citrus, cotton, tobacco and vegetables. The resulting glut on the markets and the deflation associated with the panic caused many to take losses on their harvests and forced many farmers to default on loans. The availability of easy credit prior to the panic had led many of them to borrow heavily to purchase farm tools, equipment, seed and additional land to put into production for vegetables and citrus. However, by the beginning of 1894, it was obvious even to Florida's normally booster-oriented press that times were going to be harder in the future. The Bradenton-based *Manatee River Journal* clearly saw the problem coming and warned of even higher freight rates adding to the strain:

> *For provisions, grain, fertilizer, farming tools, crate materials and interest on loans, we are seriously in debt beyond any time in the past with the next three months, taxes must be paid. On account of the poverty of the North this winter, there is every reason to expect prices of vegetables will be disastrously behind in proportion. And out of that what do we get, we must pay about $10,000 higher freight than last year.*

Since the Plant railroad had just increased shipping rates and held a virtual monopoly on transportation for the region, it was soon the object of farmers' hatred and distrust. Manatee native M.E. Gillette, who was Tampa's mayor in 1898, attempted to organize growers' cooperatives throughout the state, but after some initial successes, he found that the pressures put on farmers by traditional lenders for repayment of debts forced most of them to abandon the idea of cooperatives. The results in Florida, as in other southern states, were increased foreclosures, more unemployment and more people attempting to return to subsistence farming with little or no success. Then things got worse.

The sudden rise of the Populist Party, with its backing by white tenant farmers, small landowners and many black sharecroppers and tenant farmers, raised an old alarm among the dominant class of white landowners and business operators. The dominant Bourbon faction soon raised the cry of "black domination" in almost every political campaign at all levels. The traditional "white supremacy" argument almost always triumphed in the southern politics of the day. Blacks knew they were on the short end of political power, especially when the "Force Bill plank" was defeated at the Ocala Convention of the Populist Party. The plank, which called for the enforcement of rights put in the constitution after the Civil War, was put forth by the Negro Alliance, the Colored Farmers Alliance and the Cooperative Union. Its defeat at the convention meant to most blacks that the "White Alliance" would not back any commitment to protect blacks' right to vote. This injection of the race issue into every level of politics diverted many from exercising their rights and increased the tensions within the state and nation.

These tensions increased dramatically with the freeze of 1894–95. Those who had gambled on the continued prosperity of the citrus industry, large and small, had their hopes dashed by the weather. The freeze killed nearly every plant in Florida as far south as the Orlando area and some places farther south. As the freeze wiped out the holdings of large and small growers, many were left unemployed, deeply in debt and without any other place to go. They looked to the old fallback jobs of citrus picking, tie cutting, turpentining, lumbering and mining. It was in these same areas of employment that most of the state's black population found work. But the death of the trees became reflected in the actions taken against those who held what few menial jobs remained, i.e. blacks. Beatings of "tramps" were reported in Ocala and St. Augustine, and racial violence raised its ugly head in Key West. Allegedly random shootings began taking place in crosstie-cutting camps, and beatings were reported in the Palmetto-area citrus groves.

The conflicts were direct and sometimes very dramatic, leading to race riots and shootings. One of the first such incidents took place near Westville, in

Holmes County, where the Graves and Beatty lumber firm employed a large workforce to harvest timber. It set up temporary housing in old railroad cars along its tram railroad for the workers to use. On September 8, 1895, the workers awoke to find "leaden missiles" flying about the cars, and death and destruction within, as masked assailants fired indiscriminately into the cars. The attackers quickly fled the area when the crew supervisor showed up with other men to investigate the noise, but they left behind two dead men and many others wounded. However, as the supervisor later reported, he could get only a few men to come back to work in the area, and most of the workers fled to safety in nearby towns and cities.

A similar incident took place along the Ocklawaha River in Marion County near Moss Bluff when the camp of African American crosstie cutters was fired upon by a number of white shooters. The blacks had been on the job for less than twenty-four hours when this incident took place, and they got the message and fled. White workers, identified by the *Florida Times-Union* to be the perpetrators of the shootings, soon showed up to take their place. Blacks taken to Fort Myers also found trouble, not employment, awaiting them when they arrived in that town on the steamer *Lawrence* for the purpose of picking the citrus in the area. The labor speculator who had organized the trip was met at the wharf by eight prominent citizens and told that white laborers were welcomed, but not the black ones. Shortly thereafter, some shots rang out, and everyone took cover. Soon, "something of a reign of terror" took over in Fort Myers, but no reports of deaths reached the newspapers of the state. Yet the *New York Times* reported that twelve people had drowned attempting to flee the shooting. According to this paper, there was a regular "War Against Florida Negroes" taking place in the Sunshine State, and survivors of the violence brought back circulars warning blacks to stay out of Lee County.

Such was the climate that faced the famed Buffalo Soldiers when they arrived in the state at the beginning of the Spanish-American War.

3

THE YELLOW PRESS

The number of people who have starved in Cuba will never be definitely known. It is estimated that 800,000 were driven from their homes into the cities and towns. I had it from Spanish authorities that, according to their figures, 225,000 already have perished, but it is said that the Red Cross Society is in possession of figures showing that 425,000 Cubans have died as a result of Spanish cruelty and that 200,000 more must inevitably die.
—Correspondent, Baltimore Sun, *March 24, 1898*

Martí and the junta regularly fed stories and news of Cuba to the New York media of the day, and much of it was printed. The junta also had offices in a number of cities, including New Orleans, Jacksonville, Key West, Chicago, Detroit and St. Louis. These offices and others held events, fundraisers, town hall meetings and rallies to inform American citizens and Cuban exiles of conditions in Cuba. As a result of such efforts in the 1880s and early 1890s, the cause of Cuba Libre continued to gain new supporters and sympathizers. Although many Americans had some knowledge of the efforts of Cubans to gain their independence, the proclamation of a new revolution in 1895 yielded greater newspaper coverage than ever before. The announcement came just as Joseph Pulitzer and William Randolph Hearst embarked on a war to win subscribers to their rival New York newspapers. Relying on sensational reporting, vicious editorial cartoons and using hyperbole as a hallmark, the two owners slugged it out for the hearts, minds and pennies of the reading public. Pulitzer's *New York World* and Hearst's *New York Journal* sent reporters around the globe seeking exciting and unusual stories, but it was the realm of politics and world affairs that tended to dominate the front pages of both papers.

However, yellow press alone did not make the revolution a popular cause in the United States. The impact of these New York newspapers was largely in New York City and along the eastern seaboard but not necessarily nationwide. Few other newspapers in the United States followed the lead of the New York papers in supporting the cause of Cuba Libre. Most papers favored the cautious policies of the McKinley administration. Few Americans wanted to rush into a war without a substantial and just cause.

The *World* and *Journal* may not have been steering the thinking of most Americans, but their constant stream of stories did establish the Cuban revolution as an important international event. What really benefited the cause of Cuba Libre was the growth of the newspaper medium itself during this era. Innovations in printing, transportation and photography and the expansion of telegraph lines to even the remotest parts of the world led to a period of rapid growth of newspapers. The emergence of a large and highly literate population that demanded more news and entertainment saw the creation of thousands of new newspapers, including some that printed several new issues, or "extras," each day as developing events—murders, wars, political scandals—provided fresh news. As late as 1900, the United States had an urban population of only 30 percent, but its literacy rate was near 88 percent. There were, according to media historian John Tebbel, nearly fourteen thousand weekly newspapers and around nineteen hundred dailies. Approximately 25 percent of the nation's population over the age of ten read newspapers and magazines on a regular basis. The American population was literate and informed; indeed, the United States was one of the most literate nations in the world. The high literacy rate and thirst for knowledge many Americans evidenced made spreading the word about the Cuban cause much easier than it might have been. This thirst was sated somewhat by the creation and growth of syndicated news groups, like the Associated Press and Reuters, which made obtaining world news easier and more available.

When the Spanish navy, patrolling the waters off Cuba, fired on the American merchant ship *Allianca* in 1895, few Americans knew that a new Cuban revolution was underway. Even those Americans who were aware of the latest Cuban effort to overthrow their Spanish rulers thought that the new revolution was just like so many others in the past—of little concern to most Americans, unless they lived in Florida and were associated with the cigar or cattle industry. However, as this incident gained press coverage, more and more Americans were alarmed that Spain would fire on an unarmed American vessel in international waters. It was one thing to put down a revolution but quite another to fire on an American ship. It took the Spanish government two months to apologize for the incident and to accept responsibility for its navy's actions. About the same time, a number of Cuban-American citizens were arrested in Cuba and charged with treason and espionage. Many of those arrested at the time were newly sworn American citizens who had returned to the island to assist in the revolution against Spain.

The cases of Julio Sanguilly, a Dr. Ruiz and others soon aroused some outrage, especially when Dr. Ruiz died in prison. The American public was curious about these cases, but many people were also puzzled about their importance. Florida senator Wilkerson Call presented petitions from the citizens of Florida protesting the actions of Spanish authorities and calling for the federal government to take action on their behalf. Although the incidents made headlines in Florida and Senator Call demanded action, the rest of the nation did not get overly excited by these events. Neither the *Allianca* episode nor the imprisonment of U.S. citizens, at least at this point, made much of an impression on the American public. However, the incidents did serve to make Americans more aware of the growing seriousness of the situation in Cuba and triggered rounds of discussion and debate on what potential responses were available to the United States.

Newspaper coverage of events in Cuba increased, and frequent reports of Cuban victories against the Spanish army and loyalists soon began appearing in more and more American newspapers and magazines. The glowing reports of battlefield successes by the revolutionary forces left many readers with the impression that this Cuban revolution might actually succeed and that a republic would be established. The junta, well aware of this feeling (it provided many of these reports), made sure that shadow democratic provincial governments were formed almost as soon as they were cleared of Spanish forces.

Attitudes in the United States began to change as many Americans saw similarities between the Cuban revolution and their own struggles against the British. This image of "David versus Goliath" was a constant theme of propaganda put out by the junta and its sympathizers. Many Americans, at least by 1896, began to believe it was time for Spain to leave Cuba for good. Others, looking at the options available to the American government, believed that although the revolution might succeed, the United States had nothing to gain by becoming involved. A third position put forth in the press was that the United States should do everything in its power to bring the revolution to a close, peacefully if possible. Americans had some large investments in Cuba, and in the minds of most Americans, these investments deserved the protection of the United States government. Options on the course of American policy became frequently debated topics, especially on slow news days. Two things appear certain from reading the newspapers and magazines of the day. First, most Americans agreed that the Cuban people deserved their sympathy; and second, the Spanish would not be successful in putting this rebellion down.

As Americans became more aware of the Cuban revolution, Congress, in late 1895 and early 1896, was bombarded by 164 petitions from all over the United States requesting that the United States grant belligerent status to the revolutionaries. This, if granted, would mean that the United States recognized that a state of war existed on the island and that Americans could sell arms, ammunition and medical supplies to the rebel army. A concurrent resolution was introduced in the Senate by Senator Call of Florida, and on February 28, 1896, it was passed by that body. The House of Representatives soon followed suit, and the final version was approved by both houses on April 6, 1896. President Grover Cleveland chose to ignore the resolution and remained firm in his belief that the United States had little business

General Valeriano Weyler's policy of *reconcentrado*, or the movement of the Cuban countryside into fenced fortifications controlled by Spanish troops, made him a despised man to most Americans. This William A. Rogers painting for a major American magazine, *Harper's*, offered Rogers's view of the misery suffered by the Cuban people. *Courtesy of the Florida Historical Society.*

involving itself in the revolution. Nearly every newspaper and magazine in the country followed the debates on this topic, making Cuba the most important issue of the day.

After 1895, more and more American newspapers featured articles on the conflict in Cuba. In January 1896, General Valeriano Weyler assumed command of Spanish forces in Cuba from the ineffective General Martínez Campos. Weyler quickly realized that traditional military tactics would not succeed against the revolutionary force, which often visited small towns and villages at night and was supplied with food and drink by the populace. He decided that drastic measures were needed to deprive the rebels of these

Another William A. Rogers painting for *Harper's* depicted Spanish soldiers as cruel barbarians driving poor Cuban peasants from their homes into *reconcentrado* camps. *Courtesy of the Florida Historical Society.*

sources, and he ordered Spanish soldiers to build high fences and deep ditches around some towns. These concentration camps became the hallmark of his new *reconcentrado* strategy. Shortly after the camps had been finished and garrisoned by Spanish soldiers, Weyler issued an edict for all Cubans:

> *I order and command all the inhabitants of the country now outside of the line of fortification of the towns, shall, within the period of eight days, concentrate themselves in the town so occupied by the troops. Any individual who after the expiration of this period is found in the uninhabited parts will be considered a rebel and tried as such.*

His policy, while sound militarily, resulted in what has been called the "Cuban Holocaust." Some 1.6 million Cubans were forced to leave their villages and homes and take up residence in one of these camps. Within a few weeks after the new policy was put into place, more than 200,000 Cubans, mostly peasants, were dead. Eventually, some 480,000 would die before the policy was abandoned.

An estimated 200,000 Cubans perished because of the *reconcentrado* policies of Weyler. In this photograph, an unknown man inspects a skull in the huge pile of bones. *Courtesy of the Florida Historical Society.*

Weyler's brutal relocation policy was grist for the mills of the yellow press. All the major newspapers in the United States sent correspondents to Cuba to report on the *reconcentrado* program and to graphically portray the horrors it brought to the Cuban people. Weyler was quickly given the nickname "Butcher" and vilified on front pages across the United States. Lurid headlines proclaimed the concentration camps to be centers of rape, murder and even cannibalism as food became increasingly scarce. Once the major newspapers devoted space to this inhumane policy, they were followed by smaller papers, which often simply reprinted the stories that appeared in the larger papers. Other stories reported Spanish atrocities on the battlefield. Seldom did American newspapers have anything positive to say about Spanish authorities and soldiers.

Were the reports in the yellow press a deliberate attempt to persuade Americans of the need to go to war to liberate Cuba? Not at first, but by 1897 the tenor of the press reportage had changed from sensationalistic reporting to outright advocacy; from reporting news to making news. The best illustration of this is the story told about William Randolph Hearst, who sent the artist Frederic Remington to Cuba to draw pictures of the battles between Cuban insurrectionary forces and the Spanish army. After a short time on the island, Remington sent Hearst a telegram stating, "There is no war. Request to be recalled." Hearst allegedly responded, "Please remain. You furnish the pictures, I'll furnish the war." And he set about doing just that, devoting as many as eight pages in a single edition of the *Journal* to the Cuban situation. Other publishers followed his lead. When the United States finally declared war on Spain, Hearst crowed, "This is the *Journal's* war." Perhaps that went too far, but some of the responsibility for the war fell squarely on the shoulders of the yellow press.

As Americans became fascinated with the Cuban struggle for independence, Florida played host to a growing group of reporters who represented a large number of newspapers and magazines throughout the world. Many of these reporters had large reputations and egos to match. Most prominent were those hired by the New York papers, including the likes of Richard Harding Davis, Frederic Remington, Ralph Paine, Sylvester Scovel, George Rea and Stephen Crane. Both Paine and Crane wrote about the filibustering, and not surprisingly, both suffered some physical discomfort for their adventures. Paine was stranded on No Name Key for two weeks and had to deal with all the key's insects and vermin, while Crane suffered a shipwreck and survival-at-sea experience. Many of the reporters sent to Jacksonville wound up at the St. James Hotel and were frequent "guests" at the Hotel de Dream, run by the sophisticated madam Cora Taylor. While there, Crane and Taylor became well acquainted and remained in close contact until his death a few years later. Paine, Scovel and a host of others frequented the St. James Hotel so often that some of their contemporaries dubbed them the "St. James Gang."

Many of the New York reporters also received special treatment from Horatio Rubens when in the Big Apple, and they often called at his office, which they dubbed the "Peanut Club" because of the supply of peanuts he kept on hand. Rubens often supplied leads to Florida locations where the reporters could pick up more information about filibustering expeditions, especially those that left Tampa and Key West. Many reporters stayed in Key West, happy to frequent the offices of Western Union, which offered regular communications with Cuba. Many stories came from this connection; some were real, but some were the products of the overactive imaginations of bored, but well-paid, correspondents.

Not all correspondents lived in Florida's cities. Some, like Murat Halstead, had to live in the Inglaterra Hotel in Havana. Here, the "deprived" correspondent of the *New York Journal* lived in a choice room with glass doors opening onto a private marble balcony. His "squalid" bed had a headboard with inlaid mother of pearl and a canopy of red velvet. When he rang the bell above the headboard, it took an "impossible" 150 seconds for the servant to arrive and take his breakfast order. Five long and exhausting minutes later, the servant would return with silver pitchers of hot cream and hot coffee, a sweet roll and peeled fruit. After partaking of fresh fish, probably red snapper, prepared with a thick, red tomato sauce, which he considered too heavy, he would relax as best he could with the choicest of the island's freshest fruits. However, this severe test of the reporter's ability to survive the harsh conditions in Havana ended when General Valeriano Weyler became governor of the island.

Weyler arrested Halstead's assistant, Charles Michelson, a personal favorite of William Randolph Hearst, because Michelson had the audacity to write that the reason the revolution was still a going concern was that "Spanish soldiers do not fight." At first, Halstead and the *Journal* did not believe the story to be worth reporting—until the rival *World* got hold of the news. The brutal arrest of an American journalist was easy news to report, much easier than attempting to follow Gomez or Garcia in the jungles, and so the story hit the stands and created an immediate uproar in the United States, or at least in New York and Washington. Ten days later, Michelson was released from his Morro Castle cell and soon left the island. Spain could not afford a war with the United States over the arrest of bothersome reporters. Michelson contacted the junta representative in Key West, José

Delores Poyo, and soon more stories in a similar vein hit the wires. The fate of reporters, American citizens and others arrested and mistreated by the Spanish authorities in Cuba soon made the headlines and became the subject of extended debates in Congress.

The killing of political prisoners was also widely reported. In one instance, reported by the *New York World* and copied nationwide by other papers, the Spanish authorities emptied the jail near San Cristobal and executed all of the prisoners, including thirty sick and wounded. To cover their tracks, the soldiers set fire to the buildings and cremated the remains.

Of all the reports filtering through Florida to the north, however, few had the impact on public opinion that the sensational stories of Spanish atrocities against the civilian population in Cuba did. The executions of filibusterers trying to smuggle military equipment and men onto the island grabbed the attention of readers, but they failed to generate the same anger that stories of "Heartless Spaniards" butchering noncombatants, including women and children, did. The *Tampa Morning Tribune* reported that "Butcher" Weyler was "After Women" for lewd and demeaning purposes. According to the story, a certain Señora Martinez and her fifteen-year-old daughter, Inez, obeyed General Weyler's order to abandon the countryside and showed up at a Spanish camp. There the women were verbally abused and then stripped in front of the soldiers. Later, Inez was forced to march naked in front of the column as they proceeded through the jungle, enduring the soldiers' loud and obnoxious remarks about her appearance. Sensational stories such as this were reprinted not only in New York but also in many other newspapers throughout the nation. Like the frontier tales of rape and slaughter by American Indians, many of them were the products of the imaginations of reporters who otherwise had no stories to file.

Richard Harding Davis, reporting from Cuba and finding little to report but the arrogance of Spanish officers and officials, finally got a juicy story for Hearst when, upon boarding the Plant Line steamer *Olivette*, he witnessed three young ladies being arrested on suspicion of smuggling letters to the junta. The women, among whom was a Señorita Arango, were taken below deck and strip-searched by a female officer. Davis filed his report but did not specifically say that women were searched on deck, nor did he mention the matron who conducted the search. When Frederic Remington was asked to illustrate the story, he took the liberty of tying one of the young girls in the picture to a mast on the top deck and having her strip-searched in front of male officers, who appropriately were pictured leering at the young lady. The editors at the *World* noticed the discrepancy and sent a reporter to interview the embarrassed young lady, who quickly clarified the report. Davis was beside himself with anger over the misrepresentation and even wrote a letter to the editor explaining the circumstances and disassociating himself from the story. However, the story was out, and little could be done to change the public's first impression. Indeed, the report was vague enough to be somewhat open to the interpretation Remington gave to the episode in his drawing. It created a sensation but definitely was not true.

The celebrated arrest and escape of Evangelina Cosio de Cisneros made headlines for a longer period than the Arango affair. Old Cuban hand George Bryson, working for the *New York Journal*, found out that a convent-educated young lady was being held captive by the Spanish in the Casa de Recojidas, a somewhat notorious women's prison filled with prostitutes and psychologically unbalanced and murderous women. When Bryson and fellow journalist

Evangelina Cisneros became a popular heroine in the yellow press. Her story provided months of front-page copy. *Courtesy of the Florida Historical Society.*

George Clarke Musgrave attempted to visit the young lady, they found the place filled with filthy and naked women parading around the courtyard. The reporters were shocked to see this and called on Fitzhugh Lee, American consul in Havana, to see what he could do. Lee visited the young lady and found her isolated from the rest of the population and in a comfortable private room. According to the reports, "Miss Cisneros"—reporters always used this name to identify her because of her relationship with one of the early revolutionary leaders in the Ten Years' War—was arrested for resisting the lewd advances of one Colonel Berritz, commander of the Isle of Pines, her home district. The Hearst papers set out to make her famous as the "Cuban Joan of Arc" and helped to organize mass protest meetings in New York and elsewhere. Famed reporter James Creelman was assigned the duty of organizing these meetings and getting the story in front of the American public.

Consul Fitzhugh Lee was embarrassed by all the attention Miss Cisneros received, particularly since it came when Weyler was leaving the island and a new governor was appointed to take his place. Hearst went even further and employed men to break her out of jail. Three days after the daring jailbreak, she was smuggled aboard the steamer *Seneca*, whisked away to Florida and then hustled to New York. She was an instant celebrity and went on a nationwide speaking tour, where she detailed the horrors of life in Cuba under the Spanish. Adding luster to her name was the well-financed public sympathy of Mrs. Jefferson Davis, long in the pay of the Hearst newspapers, whose support was effective in counterbalancing the complaints of Lee. After the speaking tour, Miss Cisneros was abandoned by Hearst. She fell in love with one of her rescuers, Carlos Carbonell, and married him in May 1898. After the war, the couple returned to Cuba, where Carbonell practiced dentistry for many years.

In 1899, George Clarke Musgrave published a book, *Under Three Flags in Cuba*, which included his version of the Evangelina Cisneros saga:

> *Without warning, her father was seized, and shut in the protectorado. Half divining the reason of the persecution, Evangelina went to Berritz and begged for her father's release. The governor, gallantly assuring her that he could refuse her nothing, ordered his liberation. Trembling with joy, the frail girl poured out effusive thanks, but her heart sank when the roué continued: "Thanks are easy, but later I will judge your gratitude" and he then made violent protestation of love. From that day Evangelina remained closely indoors, and her father, realizing her danger, seldom left her.*

After the inspection of prisoners on July 24, he was again placed under arrest but his daughter, realizing what the persecution implied, did not venture into the brutal officer's presence. Two nights later, she had retired, when a knock came at the door. In hope for her father, in fear of her tormentor, she slipped on a dressing gown, when the door opened and Berritz in full uniform entered. Trembling with fear, she asked her visitor to be seated, and he inquired why she spurned him when she knew her parent's fate was in his hands.

She pitifully begged him to cease molesting her, and prayed him to release her father; but he swore he was devoted to her, threatened and cajoled alternately, and became so persistent in his attentions that she dashed for the door. The colonel seized her by the shoulders, and stifling her screams, forced her back to the inner room. But her cry for help had been heard. In the hotel, near by, some men were gathered, and rushed to the rescue. One, a young Cuban named Betencourt, was an ardent admirer of Evangelina; and with him were Vargas, a clerk, and a young French merchant named Superville. Without ceremony, they rushed into the house, seized Berritz, and flung him to the ground. Betencourt, not unnaturally, thrashed him soundly, and then he was bound with rope to be taken to the civil judge.

At first the craven cur begged for mercy; then, seeing soldiers standing undecided in the crowd, he shouted for the guard, yelling that the Cuban prisoners were murdering him. From the Cuartel a company of troops doubled up, and the people scattered. They fired down the street killing and wounding several, and then released Berritz and seized Evangelina and her three rescuers. The governor thought it politic to hush up the matter, but unfortunately, prominent citizens had been shot, and an inquiry was imminent. That he was found in a lady's room he was powerless to deny, but he excused himself by saying Evangelina had enticed him to enter, and the men, hiding inside, were ready to kill him, free the prisoners, and seize the island. The story was ludicrous, but rebellion is always scented in Cuba, and Weyler ordered the prisoners brought to Havana for trial for attempted murder and rebellion.

As historian of the foreign press's role in the Spanish-American War, Joyce Milton noted, "It was a shameful early example of the manufactured celebrity."

STATE OF NEW YORK,
CITY AND COUNTY OF NEW YORK,

Be it Remembered, That on the *Fifteenth* day of *October*
In the year of our Lord one thousand eight hundred and ninety *seven* personally
appeared *Evangelina Cosio y Cisneros*
In the *Supreme Court of the State of New York, First Judicial District,*
(said Court being a Court of Record, having common law jurisdiction, a Clerk and a Seal,)
and made *her* Declaration of Intention to become a Citizen of the United States of
America, In the words following, to wit:

"I, *Evangelina Cosio y Cisneros*
do declare on oath, that *it* is bona fide my Intention to become a Citizen of the United
States of America, and to renounce forever, all allegiance and fidelity to any foreign
Prince, Potentate, State or Sovereignty whatever, and particularly to the *Queen* of
Spain of whom I am *now a* subject, (and that
I arrived in the United States on the *12* day of *Oct* 18 *97*

Sworn, this *15* day *Evangelina Cosio y Cisneros*
of *October* 189 *7*
Residence, *Waldorf Hotel*
N. Y. City.

John H Laos
Asst. Special Deputy Clerk.

In Attestation Whereof, and that the foregoing is a true copy of the
original Declaration of Intention remaining of record in my office, I,
HENRY D. PURROY, Clerk of the said Court, have hereunto
subscribed my name and affixed the seal of the said Court, this *15*
day of *October* 189 *7*

Henry Purroy Clerk

Like many Cuban exiles, Evangelina Cisneros applied for and was granted citizenship in the United States. She later returned to Cuba with her new husband. *Courtesy of the Florida Historical Society.*

While the story of Evangelina received extensive coverage across the nation, it did not bring the United States any closer to war with Spain. It was fun reading, but readers retained a healthy skepticism about its truthfulness.

The junta and its American ally, the Cuban League, played a large role in spreading propaganda about Spanish oppression of the regular Cuban population. Even before the official arrival of General Weyler, the press in America received hundreds of press releases from Cuban groups predicting that blood would flow in the streets and calling Weyler a heartless slayer of women and children. The Spanish government played into the hands of the junta when it announced that the new governor would be given a free hand to adopt a more drastic policy than that of his predecessor. Known from his previous service in Cuba as a hard and sometimes cruel man, Weyler was a marked target for revolutionary propaganda. Almost from the moment of his arrival, Weyler stated that his policy would be more severe and, in February 1896, announced his *reconcentrado* policy, whereby citizens who lived in any area controlled by the Spanish were required to relocate around the local military headquarters. No passes were to be issued unless approved by the local commander; commercial establishments were to be controlled by the local military authorities; and all persons were required to be at the service of the local military should they be called upon. Essentially, this policy amounted to house arrest for the entire population living under Spanish control.

The problems of feeding, clothing and sheltering such a concentration of people were hardly considered, and the rising death toll, regularly reported in many American newspapers, shocked an already sympathetic public. The yellow press in New York had a field day reporting the horrors created by this policy, as did a number of Florida papers with correspondents in Cuba. Efforts by Weyler to censor stories filed by reporters failed to stop the outward flow of damaging stories, and he eventually expelled most reporters from the United States or confined them to restricted areas.

Many reports of life in the *reconcentrado* camps were smuggled to Key West, where the local telegraph office kept a steady stream of stories flowing to the nation's papers. Some reporters, like James Creelman, who had been ordered off the island, refused to go and sent out secret reports via various means, particularly on the Plant System's steamer *Olivette*, which had a regular route between Tampa and Havana, with frequent stopovers in Key West. Henry Plant ordered his ship's personnel to keep watch on the situation in Cuba, gather information about conditions and pass the information to United States military authorities. General Weyler's order to shoot Cubans who remained outside the *reconcentrado* fences was published in American newspapers before some of his own troops learned of it. Of course, not all of the atrocities written up by the reporters were completely true, but reports of large numbers of Cubans dying at the hands of Spanish soldiers, confirmed by Spanish authorities, struck a chord of sympathy in the American public. Reporters and editors could always rely on stories about the ill treatment of women and children at the hands of Weyler's "fiends" to sell newspapers.

The number of exaggerated stories planted by junta operatives is difficult to ascertain. George Auxier, one of the first historians to study the activities of the junta and to evaluate the impact of yellow journalism on areas outside New York, observed that many of the atrocity stories did originate with the reporters of American newspapers but cautioned that many could be traced "to the hand of Estrada Palma and the members of the Junta, who, until war was declared in April 1898, received the cooperation of the editors in depicting

Spanish barbarities through editorial, cartoon, and verse." The fact that members of Congress cited many of the stories in speeches on the situation makes it clear that they did have an impact beyond the normal readership.

A follow-up study by J. Stanley Lemons found that many of the smaller country papers did not follow the trend to publish the atrocity stories, and had it not been for the establishment of "ready-print" news bureaus like the Associated Press, few stories about the Cuban situation might ever have reached small-town America at all. Not until the arrival of "Butcher" Weyler did the small-town presses of the Midwest pay much attention to Cuba. However, even Weyler's activities did not change the opinion of most people in that region about going to war for Cuba. Many of the small-town editors saw the stories as products of "war producers" in the East. The junta, in offices in Detroit, St. Louis, Kansas City and elsewhere, tried hard to convince the population of the justness of its cause and gradually succeeded. However, most Americans just did not see Cuban independence as something that merited intervention by the United States. That would have to come after a direct attack on American interests or citizens.

Florida newspapers initially did not jump on the sensationalist bandwagon and played down this aspect of the revolution. While Tampa papers had every reason to join their New York colleagues, most of their front-page stories were limited to accounts of the fighting in Cuba. Atrocities by both sides were reported, but not in the sensational style of the Hearst or Pulitzer papers. One of the more sensational stories published in the *Tampa Tribune* dealt with the killing of thirty unarmed Cubans in Pinar del Rio at Guanabacoa. The article, which carried a New York byline, went into some detail of the murders ordered by the Spanish commander and included descriptions of the lewd actions of some soldiers toward women in the group. When the group attempted to flee, the Spanish soldiers fired, and those who were wounded or who surrendered were bound, gagged and shot. The officer in charge, Colonel Fondeviela, then ordered his men not to bury the bodies but to let the buzzards have a feast. The American consul, Fitzhugh Lee, and the bishop of Havana went to the scene and interceded to see to the proper burial of the dead. Since much the same story is reported in Lee's formal reports, the event seems to have been genuine. At the same time, the *Tribune* was one of the first papers to dismiss, through Lee's statements and those of Henry Plant and others, the alleged strip-search on the *Olivette*, as depicted by the Remington illustration, as pure fantasy. That the Tampa papers kept close tabs on the revolution is not surprising, but their failure to utilize the sensational style of the yellow press in reporting events in Cuba is certainly unusual.

The *Ocala Banner*, serving an inland town with a suburb known as Martí City, also did not follow the route of yellow journalism. When the paper reported on the revolution at all, it was in the context of fundraising by Estrada Palma or Mayor Cuesta of Martí City or excursions by cigar workers to Jacksonville or some other place to hear Cuban spokesmen. Like almost all newspapers in Florida, the most fascinating topic for *Banner* readers was the successes or failures of filibusterers. The *Levy Times-Democrat*, at least in the few surviving issues available, usually reported one-paragraph pieces: "There is considerable guess work in the Spanish Statement that they could conquer Florida with 100,000 men. The man who made that estimate was not familiar with the job." In their October 31, 1895 edition, the same paper noted, "There has been little change in the Cuban situation, but it is generally believed that a crisis of some kind is not far off...At any rate, the islanders are contending against great odds, and the outcome of the struggle will be watched with keen interest." The editors of most of the smaller weekly newspapers and a majority of the dailies in Florida adopted an attitude of wait and see, not sensationalism and conquest by war.

On the Atlantic coast of Florida, the *Florida Star*, published in Titusville, ran one of its first pieces on March 8, 1895, noting that Spain enforced an oppressive system of rule that was designed to make Spaniards rich at the expense of Cubans. "It seems strange," a special correspondent wrote, "that the home government cannot understand that there is no surer way of killing the golden egg laying goose than to starve and maltreat it, yet that is exactly the course pursued toward Cuba." The writer went on to note that only one-fifth of the most fertile island in the Caribbean was under cultivation and that Cubans had no respect for the colonial government, primarily because it was so corrupt. Later, in 1897, the same paper reported on the decision of General Gomez to fight fire with fire by dynamiting trains and hospitals caring for the wounded, just as Weyler had ordered his troops to do to the insurgents. The paper deplored this attitude but quoted Sherman's famous statement on war and moved on to other topics. The paper was concerned about the McKinley administration's Cuban policy, which it hoped would be stronger than Grover Cleveland's. It chided the new Republican administration for taking so little action toward the Cuban situation but at the same time seemed willing to annex Hawaii, over two thousand miles from the Pacific coast of the United States.

In the newly founded city of Miami, the *Miami Metropolis* seemed content to note the many filibustering expeditions and cheer them on but insisted that Spain should pick up the tab for patrolling its own waters around Cuba, "instead of burdening Uncle Sam with the expense of patrolling our coast line and preventing the supplies to Cuba." The *Metropolis* did publish one syrupy romantic story about Margareta, the daughter of a Señor Dominguez, who fell in love with a suitor recently arrived from Cuba. When the father inquired when the suitor came to Key West, the daughter stated that he had been exiled there six months ago. The father, a true Cuban patriot, wondered why the young man had not returned to Cuba to free it from Spanish oppression. When the daughter dutifully answered she did not know, her father told her to quit seeing such a man, who lacked courage to fight for his country's freedom. The young man, Emmanuel, returned to Cuba and was killed crossing one of the *trochas* (trenches) fighting for Cuba's freedom. In true melodramatic fashion, the story ended with: "Night and the stars! Ah, how cold they were—the stars, the Trocha and Emmanuel. Emmanuel, Emmanuel! It was for Cuba Libre." As the war approached, the Flagler-run paper simply pushed hard for the establishment of a torpedo boat station to be placed in Miami and, of course, cheered on the filibusterers.

As the only newspaper that could claim a more statewide audience, the *Florida Times-Union* of Jacksonville offered more coverage of the Cuban situation than any of the other Florida papers. With both the *Dauntless* and the *Three Friends* frequently operating out of the port of Jacksonville, the emphasis of the coverage was on filibusterers and their plights. The newspaper also took advantage of J.A. Huau's frequent press releases, most of which dealt with the actions of the revolutionary army and the cost of the war on Spain's notoriously weak treasury. The *Times-Union* also followed the Cisneros case closely and reported the jubilation of the Cuban community when she was freed. More evenhanded than its New York brethren, the Jacksonville paper also reported when the revolutionary army suffered losses or defeat at the hands of the Spaniards. The *Times-Union* followed the saga of General Weyler as his policies continued to fail in the face of the persistent revolutionary armies. Editorially, the Democratic *Times-Union* supported McKinley's efforts to get Spain to accept the good offices of the United States in ending the revolution and noted that the policy was doomed to failure if there were no real changes in the Spanish government's attitudes and actions—a prediction that proved to be accurate.

Overall, the Florida press was hesitant to demand United States involvement in Cuban affairs and followed the line set by both President Cleveland and President McKinley. The American Civil War had occurred just over thirty short years earlier when the revolution broke out in Cuba, and there were thousands of veterans who had been through the horrors of that war who were reluctant to send their sons or grandsons off to some hostile environment to fight for someone else's freedom, no matter how right or wrong. "Major" McKinley sensed this feeling and refused to commit American forces until circumstances forced a different solution. Florida newspapers generally agreed with him and argued that nonmilitary involvement was the correct policy to follow. Only two newspapers, both small and relatively insignificant, pushed for military involvement—the Bradenton-based *Manatee River Journal*, whose editor was running for political office and needed a platform, and the Key West paper, which was so full of stories created in the editor's imagination that even the reporters loitering around the telegraph office refused to believe it.

The conservative stances of the newspapers of Florida reflected positions taken by the majority of newspapers throughout the country, with the notable exceptions of the Hearst, Pulitzer and one or two other major dailies. With the sinking of the *Maine* in Havana Harbor in February 1898, opinions changed rapidly. American lives had been lost, and no one was safe.

4

THE FLORIDA EXPERIENCE

Filibusterers and Politicians

FERNANDINA, Fla., January 12 (1895)—This place was thrown into great excitement today by the seizure of the steam yacht Lagonda, *as she was about leaving port, by the United States customs officials. The vessel was detained in obedience to orders from Washington, which stated that she was bound on a filibustering expedition.*
—Florida Times-Union, *January 13, 1895*

Florida, like much of the Midwest and newly established territories in the Far West, was basically rural and had only three cities worthy of that name. Jacksonville, Key West and Tampa were the largest centers of population and also had the largest share of the Cuban emigrant population. All three were centers of cigar manufacturing and related industries. Florida's rural population reflected many traits similar to the rest of the nation in that it was served by a number of weekly newspapers while the cities noted above had at least one daily newspaper available. The state did not have any dominant newspaper and only one that could claim something approaching a statewide circulation, the *Florida Times-Union and Citizen.* Nevertheless, William Schellings noted many years ago, "The newspapers of Florida...were seemingly unaffected by the spirit of jingoism that affected so many other papers."

The overall reporting was very friendly toward the Cuban cause but was not overly active in pushing intervention in the war. For the larger papers of the three cities mentioned above, part of the reason for this cautious approach was the power of the cigar manufacturers, many of whom were Spanish, while the workforce was mainly Cuban. Newspapers, then as now, responded to their advertisers and not always to the readership. The rural areas of the state were hardly affected by the revolution and were interested, at first, only as observers, not as participants. No one in Florida, it should be noted, wanted the annexation of Cuba as an alternative to intervention. Cuba produced too many products similar to those grown in Florida, sugar being the prime example, but Florida also produced tobacco, cotton and pineapples, which were the main exports of Cuba as well. Florida's long history of profitable trade with Cuba was also a mitigating factor, especially in the southern portion of the state, where the cattle industry had a long and very substantial trade with the island. Finally, finding a common opinion of U.S. policy toward Cuba or any other country was always difficult in substantially rural states, and Florida was no different from its western counterparts in this respect.

Florida's fame in the years during the revolution did not come from trade, the production of sugar or even the attempts of Hamilton Disston and friends to drain the Everglades. What captured the American imagination more than anything was the derring-do of filibusterers, who left bases in the Sunshine State and risked life and limb to smuggle arms, ammunition and medical supplies to the revolutionary armies of Gomez, Garcia and Maceo. Successful or not, the exploits of filibusterers such as Napoleon Bonaparte Broward, "Dynamite Johnny" O'Brien and others made headlines and stirred the souls of the adventurous. These bold men and their boats became legends in their times and were eulogized whenever one was unfortunate enough to be captured, executed or sunk on his missions. The importance of their role in generating propaganda for the Cuban cause, however, could not to be understated. Their exploits kept the public interested in reading more about them, and readers were willing to believe that they achieved even more than they actually accomplished. In truth, the number of successful voyages was far outweighed by those that did not succeed or even leave their homeports. The numbers of troops supplied via these voyages to the Cuban revolutionary army was small, though not unimportant in some instances.

Almost every vessel that left on a filibustering voyage to Cuba was funded by the junta and its allies. From the signing of the Zanjón Pact in 1878 until the outbreak of the final Revolution of 1895, the junta groups throughout the United States and many in the countries of Latin and Central America attempted to raise funds for the revolution. Bond sales were conducted in the hope that investors would be willing to take a chance on the revolution's success, even if it meant the overthrow of a recognized, legitimate government. Rallies, speeches, pamphlets and almost every means available were used to attract supporters who would help fund the revolution. All too often, expeditions were sent to Cuba only to fail, and these failures were costly to the various Cuban groups that funded them because their financial resources were limited. Recruitment of men and materials was always difficult, and the actions of the juntas were invariably under the watchful eyes of the Spanish consuls, Spanish citizens and hired detectives, like the Pinkertons.

As with all revolutions, betrayals were common, and plans had to be scrubbed at the last possible moment when backers realized that they had been compromised. Accumulating sufficient amounts of money to fund such expeditions was a constant problem for the junta in the United States, but there were always adventurers who were willing to do almost anything for the thrills of challenging authority and the faintest prospect of making large sums of money. Still, the junta had to be very careful because what was at risk were the lives of friends and family and, most importantly, the success or failure of the cause of Cuban freedom.

Martí was the preeminent fundraiser for the junta, and his appearances throughout the country were widely reported, especially those in Florida, where the supporters of the revolution in Key West and Tampa vied to contribute funds. His visits to Florida brought in thousands of dollars to the revolutionary fund, and many of the cigar workers in Tampa and Key West pledged at least one day's pay on a regular basis to fund the movement. Martí also made one of his most important contributions to the revolution during his 1892 visits to Key West and Tampa. During this fundraising drive, his conversations with colleagues and friends in these two Florida cities led to the creation of the Cuban Revolutionary Party (PRC), which he announced in Tampa.

The PRC was to be dedicated to winning complete independence for Cuba and guiding the revolution to its final, successful conclusion. The PRC was not a monolithic organization but relied on local clubs (cells) to raise funds, find volunteers and propagandize on behalf of the revolution. The success of the Florida branches of the PRC was evidenced by the fact that more money was raised in Florida than the combined total of funds raised in all other Latin or Central American countries. The Florida PRC also assumed responsibility for assisting filibusterers leaving from Florida ports by storing arms and ammunition in convenient places out of sight of the numerous Spanish spies. So successful was the PRC as an organization that Tampa alone had forty-one clubs by 1896—thirty in Ybor City and eleven in West Tampa. To promote harmony and maintain a steady flow of funding, the PRC also took a hand in curtailing strikes among the cigar workers. Many of the major cigar manufacturers also financially supported the revolutionary cause, including Ybor, Teodoro Perez and Cecilo Hernriquez in Tampa and

Eduardo Hidalgo Gato in Key West, and the PRC used its influence with workers to ensure stable labor relations. Maintaining peace in the labor force was important enough that Tomas Estrada Palma, who took over the PRC after Martí's death in 1895, came to Tampa in February 1896 to urge the cigar workers to remain on their jobs in the name of Cuba Libre. Florida was the most important source of funds for the revolution, and the PRC wanted nothing to disrupt the flow of these vital dollars.

Filibustering was a difficult and dangerous game, and Martí found out firsthand just how harrowing it could be. He attempted to take a force of men and arms to Cuba in January 1895 from the deep-water port of Fernandina. The overall plan was relatively simple. Three ships were to leave Fernandina on January 12, 1895, and head southward. The first ship was to pick up Antonio Maceo and his small band of revolutionaries; the second ship would go to Key West and take General Roloff and Serafin Sanchez on board and head straight to Cuba; and the third would sail to Santo Domingo and pick up General Gomez, with Martí, Enrique Collazo and Mayia Rodriquez on board to greet and accompany the general to Cuba. Unfortunately, Roloff and Sanchez had informed an old veteran of the Ten Years' War, Fernando Lopez de Queralta, about the upcoming invasion, and this poor soul let the secret slip. The planned invasion of Cuba from Fernandina was now jeopardized. The information was quickly passed on to the Spanish consul and then to the Spanish minister, who alerted U.S. Customs authorities of the plan.

The Cuban revolutionary groups were not very discreet in their activities and aroused the suspicions of many people in Jacksonville and Fernandina. They openly visited Nathanial Borden, their contact in Fernandina, and even signed the register at the Florida House, which left an easy-to-follow paper trail for Spain's paid informants. When Borden went to New York to assist in procuring a vessel for the expedition, he was followed closely. When he, on behalf of Martí, used the name "D.E. Mantell" to hire the vessel, it fooled no one. Even the *New York World* knew when the boats were hired and wired their correspondent in Fernandina to be on the lookout for the *Lagonda* and the *Amadis*, two vessels that had recently left New York under suspicious circumstances. The correspondent was T.E. Hall, who doubled as the county judge in Nassau County and who quickly informed the collector of customs at Fernandina, George L. Batzell.

The game was up before it ever left the port. The vessels had been loaded with eight hundred rifles and 600,000 rounds of ammunition and were to be accompanied by the Martí party. Word of the aborted mission soon hit Jacksonville, where a small group of PRC supporters took to the streets demanding that a "thunderbolt" strike the traitor who betrayed the mission. Martí and his companions left the area quickly, and their associate, José Alejandro Huau, was able to intercede and reclaim most of the guns and ammunition through his friendship with local customs officials. The failure of the *Lagonda* expedition was a tremendous disappointment and a serious drain on the junta's limited funds.

Many historians have called this aborted filibustering trip a real fiasco, but Antonio de la Cova and Paul Braun place the episode in a different light. According to Braun's study of press coverage about the event, the *Lagonda* incident resulted in tremendous publicity for the revolutionary movement and greatly enhanced its fundraising activities. Citing the opinion of Enrique Collazo, one of the leaders of the movement, Braun argues that Fernandina was not a fiasco, since money literally poured into the treasury of the PRC in the aftermath. Antonio de la Cova found that the loss of the ammunition and arms "inspired Cuban exiles and their supporters in the United States to continue the war effort by organizing numerous filibuster expeditions to the island in order to gain national independence." Thus, the fiasco turned into something more favorable than even the planners had hoped for and provided the PRC with the means to go forward with other, more discreetly disguised plans for invading Cuba. Indeed, Braun's observation that the *Lagonda* failure was a "flashpoint" is well taken.

Numerous filibustering expeditions were undertaken in the three years of the revolution, but most were not successful. In addition to the prospect of being intercepted by the Spanish navy cruising around the coasts of Cuba, filibusterers had to worry about the United States Customs Service cutters that plied the Atlantic coast to stop their adventures. Ports that could support oceangoing vessels or ships that could at least make it past the American territorial limit of three miles were used as bases for filibustering expeditions. Pensacola, Cedar Key, Tampa, the Manatee River ports, Charlotte Harbor, the Caloosahatchee River, the Keys and all the way to Jacksonville and Fernandina were home bases for filibustering expeditions. Many of them were simple enough in execution. Small boats capable of venturing past the three-mile limit were loaded with arms and supplies and sent to meet larger vessels waiting in deeper waters. Frequently, fake destinations were written on the manifests required by customs officials; then the boat would meet a larger cohort in deep water, transfer the goods and return to port. It was not uncommon for the larger vessel to have a number of volunteers aboard to assist with the transfer of cargo who would then join the revolutionary army upon their arrival in Cuba. Because it was difficult to prove that the smaller vessels had transferred troops or supplies to larger ones, these kinds of expeditions proved highly successful. So large was the scale of the operations that the junta created a Department of Expeditions under General Emilio Nunez to coordinate the numerous forays. Florida's coastal islands and multitudinous inlets made the state an ideal base for conducting such operations.

Filibustering expeditions were reported widely in the national press. One interesting cruise reported in the *Cincinnati Post* and the *Paoli* [Indiana] *News* was commanded by Fort Myers captain A.F. Gonzalez, a veteran navigator of the Caloosahatchee River and a Cuban-born American citizen. On May 14, 1896, aboard the *Gladiator*, he allegedly sailed for Cuba with arms and men right under the nose of the revenue cutter *Forward*. The vessel got all the way to Key West before it was stopped. The Key West newspaper sadly reported that none of the passengers had the opportunity to distinguish themselves in combat with the Spanish forces on the island of Cuba and lamented the fact that their expedition had brought no positive results. The paper concluded that the filibusterers would be greeted with silence when they returned to Fort Myers, with no brass band playing "Hail the Conquering Heroes" or any of the popular Sousa marches of the day. Such was the reward of the men who dared venture on a "fishing trip" of nineteen days to Miami. Fake stories, such as this one, were almost as important as the real ones because they kept the public interested in the affairs of the Cuban revolutionaries.

Two Florida-based vessels, famous for running the Spanish naval gauntlet and reaching the Cuban coast with regularity, were frequently in the headlines of the day. The *Three Friends* and the *Dauntless* were two of the fastest vessels to make the journey to Cuba and escape the vigilant Spanish navy. The *Three Friends* was built, owned and financed by three friends—brothers Napoleon and Montclam Broward and their friend George DeCottes. This seagoing tugboat was one of the most powerful boats constructed in Florida and served many years on the St. Johns River at its home port of Jacksonville. The *Three Friends* was launched on February 2, 1895, just in time to participate in the illicit trade between Florida and Cuba. The boat was christened by Hortense Broward, the sister of the Broward brothers. Napoleon was already involved in political misadventures of his own as the sheriff of Duval County. In April 1895, Governor Henry L. Mitchell removed Napoleon as sheriff, a power he had under the Florida constitution. Undaunted by the political setback of the moment, Napoleon, who would later become governor, had been contacted by Jacksonville junta leader J.A. Huau before the construction of the *Three Friends* had been completed. Huau was a trusted friend and political ally of Broward's. Embroiled in his own political fight at the time, Broward remained out of the picture until, after his failure to gain any oceangoing business in Nassau and Key West, he and his business partners decided to sign a contract with the junta.

J.M. Barrs, a highly respected and well-known Jacksonville attorney, served as the legal adviser to Broward and included some unique stipulations in the contract that he felt would allow Broward and his partners to stay marginally within the laws of the United States. After signing the contract in February 1896, their adventures began with the attempt to smuggle General Enrique Colasso and a cargo of arms and men to an ocean rendezvous with the schooner *Stephen Mallory*. Because Colasso was closely watched, and after a storm made the *Stephen Mallory's* voyage impossible, the plan changed to carrying the general to Jacksonville in secret. The story of their efforts reads like a dime novel of the period, but they did get the general to Barrs's house and soon onto the *Three Friends* at DeCottes's mill, three miles downriver from Jacksonville. Once on board, Colasso directed Broward to head for Cuba.

The federal revenue boat in the area, the *Boutwell*, was commanded by an old acquaintance of Broward's, Captain Kilgore, but was in dry dock at the time of the expedition and could not intercept the *Three Friends*. When the tug finally arrived off the coast of Cuba, the pilot sent by the junta brought the boat too close to a town occupied by a small garrison of Spanish troops. After an exciting landing under an exchange of gunfire, the *Three Friends* escaped into the open sea and by the next morning was safely resting in Key West Harbor. News of this adventure, spread in part by Spanish officials, was reported widely in newspapers nationwide. Broward, arriving in Jacksonville in his newly polished vessel and standing on the deck in his formal captain's uniform, denied being on a filibustering expedition and noted that he had taken guns and ammunition to Key West but that the parties who had contracted for them had left the harbor by the time he arrived. The story did not ring true to the Spanish consul in Jacksonville, but it mattered not since there was nothing he could do to disprove Broward's story. Over the next two years, the legend of the *Three Friends* and its now famous captain continued to grow and later helped boost him into the governorship of Florida.

Probably the most successful of the filibustering captains was "Dynamite Johnny" O'Brien, who captained a number of vessels during his long and colorful career as a filibusterer. At one time, when Broward was under close scrutiny, O'Brien commanded the *Three Friends*. He also commanded the *Commodore*, later made famous by the publication of Stephen Crane's classic story "The Open Boat," and most notably the oceangoing tug *Dauntless*. The *Dauntless* was based in Brunswick, Georgia, and had the reputation of being one of the fastest boats on the water. The junta became interested in it when Alphonso Fritot, J.A. Huau's son-in-law and an active member of the Jacksonville junta, found out that it was for sale for $30,000. William A. Bisbee, of the Jacksonville law firm of Bisbee & Foster, helped arrange for the purchase of the *Dauntless* and also arranged for a loan through his firm. Horatio Rubens, the attorney for the New York junta who often successfully defended filibusterers in court, came to Brunswick with the money in $1,000 bills stashed around his body. The deal was consummated quickly, and soon the *Dauntless* was quayside in Jacksonville. On its very first runs as a filibustering ship, the *Dauntless* was the final destination for a number of recruits and ammunition and weapons smuggled south from New York in railroad cars.

In another dime-novel kind of adventure, Fritot arranged the switching of cars at strategic points along the route—he was an employee of the Plant System and had some control of the management of rail traffic in and out of Jacksonville—leaving the detectives shadowing the cars sitting on a siding alone in the dark. One of the passengers of this voyage was Frederick Funston, soon to be one of the most famous men in the world after his capture of Philippine revolutionary leader Emilio Aguinaldo. Funston was in charge of a twelve-pound Hotchkiss gun, the first of many such field guns to be shipped to Cuba. O'Brien's success in delivering his cargo of men and equipment to Cuba placed him squarely in the front ranks of popular heroes of the day.

Like the *Three Friends*, the *Dauntless* made many voyages, and almost all of them were covered in the press. The success of these filibustering parties made it appear that the revolution was succeeding. As story after story of successful filibustering expeditions reached print, the public became more and more convinced that this time Cuba might just free itself from the Spanish yoke.

The media of the day focused much of their attention on Florida as the main base of operations of the filibustering expeditions. The *Review of Reviews*, a major magazine of the day, summed up the frustration of Spanish colonial authorities: "So long as the revolutionaries have the money to spend, it will be almost impossible to prevent the landing of arms and supplies." Even when filibusterers were arrested and tried in court, they were seldom convicted. With each failure to convict, local populations and most of the newspapers celebrated. According to Arthur Barnes, the publicity surrounding filibustering expeditions had a two-fold impact. First, the expeditions involved American citizens, and second, the expeditions provided topics for public discussion. Because they were "good copy," few newspapers refused to publish materials on these expeditions.

The noninterventionist press, like the *New York Evening Post* and the pacifist *Friends' Intelligencer and Journal*, was worried about the impact of these ventures into foreign waters. After all, they endangered American lives and put the nation into possible peril should something drastic take place, like the old *Virginius* affair of 1873, which almost resulted in war with Spain. This incident occurred when Captain Joseph Fry, his crew and passengers were captured during the Ten Years' War and taken to Santiago, where most of the fifty-five men in the expedition were executed. Thus, filibustering expeditions leaving Florida ports played a major role in keeping Cuba Libre on or near the front pages of American newspapers.

In Congress, the cause of Cuban independence had no greater advocate than Florida's senator, Wilkerson Call. He had a keen interest in the affairs of Cuba and had, as early as 1890, asked Congress to look into affairs on the island. One of his major contentions was the control of the island's finances by German bankers. Like other expansionists, he possessed a keen awareness of the growing power of Germany, and he wanted to prevent that country from gaining a strong foothold in the Caribbean. Call also felt that there might be a deal in the works to transfer ownership of Cuba to Germany in order to pay off Spain's huge debts to German bankers. Call, as a native son of Florida, knew all about the transfer of Spanish territory for purposes of paying off debts. Two years later, he asked Congress to investigate ways to improve and maintain commercial relations with the islands of the Caribbean, with a specific reference to Cuba. Later that same year, he submitted a resolution asking the president to reopen negotiations with Spain and attempt to get Spain to recognize the establishment of a Cuban republic. His resolution failed to pass on this occasion.

In 1893, Call sought another investigation into the question of immigration between Cuba and the United States. He brought up the problem of the frequent outbreaks of yellow fever, which he blamed on the passage of 50,000 to 100,000 Cubans between the island and the United States each year. He noted the increasing virulence of the disease, and he specifically lamented the daily commercial voyages between Cuban ports and Tampa and Key West, where many of the outbreaks allegedly started. As trade increased between the two countries, so, too, did outbreaks of the disease in the Sunshine State. Call asked for an increase in appropriations for the establishment of federal quarantine stations all along the Gulf Coast and up the Atlantic seaboard from Key West to South Carolina. He then persuaded the committee to ask for additional appropriations to assist other island countries and possessions in establishing "a system of international sanitation and regulation" to forestall the spread of contagious diseases. The hearings were conducted jointly with the House Committee on Immigration and Naturalization and "through subcommittees at Havana, Cuba, and at Key West, Fla." The weak Spanish administration of Cuba was a major worry for Call, and each proposal he made can be seen as an inch-by-inch assault on Spanish control of the island.

In 1895, no one outdid the senator from Florida in asking for direct intervention in the affairs of Cuba. He was joined by his Florida colleague Sam Pasco in presenting a number of petitions calling for the recognition of a state of belligerency in Cuba. On December 3, 1895, Call and Pasco submitted a resolution asking the president to protect the rights of belligerents and the Cuban revolutionists. Another resolution authored by Call asked the president to take steps to ensure that the rules of warfare were observed on both sides. He insisted that the revolution was a war between the Spanish government and the revolutionary government of Cuba, a distinction the United States had not made. Call's resolutions were pointedly hostile to Spain. He argued that the island was one of the most fertile and militarily important spots in the Caribbean and, under control of a hostile power, could hamper the trade and prosperity of the southern states of the United States, as well as other nations in the Americas. However, he argued:

> With a government properly constituted and properly administered, it would furnish a home and business for a large portion of the people of the United States. As it is, the country presents a spectacle of ruin, of misgovernment, of barbarous cruelty, which, to say the least, is a disgrace to this civilized age.

Citing a report by the House Committee on Foreign Relations, Call noted that the report was very detailed and that this august committee had recommended recognition of a state of belligerency in Cuba. He then launched into an argument for the release of General Julio Sanguilly, an American citizen and a former leader in the Ten Years' War, who had been seized by Spanish authorities in Cuba and, after a mock trial, thrown into prison with the sentence of life at hard labor. As an American citizen, Call argued, Sanguilly should have been granted all the rights and protections our government could offer. Sanguilly was just one of many who would be arrested and imprisoned on the island, and Call asked for protection of all of them.

In one of his more memorable speeches on behalf of Cuban freedom, Call noted that Cuba did not need to be annexed to the United States and that in his first resolution on the topic he had proposed the purchase, not the annexation, of the island. The purpose, he reminded his colleagues, was to give the Cubans the opportunity to join the family of nations and to do so under a government of their own choosing. In 1897, he stood in the Senate chamber to discuss the plight of Americans imprisoned in Cuba and to condemn the actions of the Spanish authorities in the case of *New York Journal* reporter Charles Govin, who reported on the revolution for many of the newspapers and had been taken prisoner by the Spanish in December. He was unarmed and had not participated in any action against Spanish forces. When he showed his citizenship papers to the commanding officer, along with his press credentials, the officer knocked them to the ground. He was tied up and bound to another prisoner; he remained for the first night in this position. The next day, according to Call's witness, Govin was taken away by a cavalry unit, tied to a tree and then used as a live dummy for saber practice and hacked to death.

Call then proceeded to inform his listeners of the fate of the dentist Dr. Battincourt, who was arrested on the streets of Havana, where he had practiced dentistry for a number of years. His crime, as best as his son could find out, was that he was found talking to a known revolutionary, which the son said was something his father had always tried to avoid. He was taken away, presumably to Morro Castle, and imprisoned. At the time of his speech, Call had received no word about the dentist's final fate. Dr. Battincourt, like Sanguilly and Govin, were American citizens, he insisted, and deserved the protection of their government.

Call then discussed the fate of one of the common sailors on the filibustering vessel *Competitor*. Here he noted that the victim was an innocent sailor who did not know the destination of the boat when he signed on as a member of the boat's crew. The Spanish navy captured the vessel, and all persons aboard the *Competitor* were imprisoned and threatened with execution. These cases and more like them, in Call's opinion, required the United States to meet its obligations to its citizens engaged in trade and commerce. Call then moved for a full investigation of these incidents. Although the motion received widespread attention in the press, it was not passed or acted upon by the incoming McKinley administration.

Call was not the only Florida political figure to demand action by the federal government. His fellow senator, Sam Pasco, and Florida representative Stephen M. Sparkman of Tampa, strongly supported his efforts. As a politician, Sparkman could ill afford to lose the Cuban vote, but politics aside, he had strong personal feelings in favor of the Cuban people's struggles against Spain. In Congress, he consistently voted to support resolutions similar to those introduced by Call and Pasco. He was certainly the source of many of the stories published in Tampa newspapers about the happenings in Congress and always received the strong support of the *Tampa Morning Tribune*. As the likelihood of war neared, Sparkman, a strong Democrat, devoted most of his energies to finding the funds necessary to fight any war and improve Florida's port facilities. However, when the question of selling bonds to fund war costs came up in Congress, his strong speech in opposition to the measure made headlines at home. Selling bonds to pay for a war was something new, and the conservative Democratic congressman could not support such an issue. However, his refusal to support the issuance of bonds did not change his support of the cause of Cuba Libre.

The newspaper coverage of congressional debates about American involvement in Cuba kept the issue in front of the American people, especially in Florida. The discussions and debates made the public aware of the instability and violence in Cuba and encouraged citizens to demand federal action to help the people of that troubled island. Petitions were sent to Congress from isolated and remote hamlets, from large cities and from small towns in the United States demanding immediate American intervention on behalf of the Cuban population. Individuals spent time and money to solicit the support of other Americans for the cause of Cuban liberty. One such request appeared in the *Levy Times-Democrat*, a rural Florida newspaper, from "the liberty-loving Dr. Miles Medical Co. of Elkhart, Ind[iana]," who asked the citizens of Bronson to sign petitions to Congress demanding the granting of belligerent status to the Cuban revolutionaries. Many congressmen, notably the brash Bourke Cockran of New York, made speeches and wrote letters to the local papers encouraging support for Cuba Libre.

Cockran, at the behest of Charles Dana of the *New York Sun*, spoke at a major rally in New York to protest against "the barbarity, butchery and rapine organized and directed by the Spanish government on the island of Cuba." The fact that the rally's sponsorship by the United Cuban Revolutionary Clubs was often not reported in the coverage of Bourke's remarks is indicative of the spirit of the times and the nature of the debate. In Congress, the debates were remarkably less partisan than would be expected. Many, like Henry Cabot Lodge, Cockran, Call and others, actually crossed party lines in voting for these resolutions and funding requests. President Grover Cleveland's staunchly held belief that it was not our fight did not sway a number of important Democrats any more than the opposition to the coming of the war by Speaker Thomas B. Reed stopped some Republicans from voting approval of the final resolutions and funding bills. If anything, the debates in Congress increased interest in the plight of Cuba and eventually won the overwhelming support of the American public.

5

PREPARATIONS FOR WAR

The American Navy

The United States has not that shield of defensive power behind which time can be gained to develop its reserve of strength. As for a seafaring population adequate to her possible needs, where is it? Such a resource, proportionate to her coast-line and population, is to be found only in a national merchant shipping and its related industries, which at present scarcely exist. It will matter little whether the crews of such ships are native or foreign born, provided they are attached to the flag, and her power at sea is sufficient to enable the most of them to get back in case of war. When foreigners by thousands are admitted to the ballot, it is of little moment that they are given fighting-room on board ship.
—Alfred T. Mahan

Writing for *Harper's Monthly Magazine* in March 1897, Captain Alfred T. Mahan made a clear distinction between preparations for war and general military preparedness. The former, wrote America's greatest naval theorist, was a question of available material and was constantly changing, whereas the latter involved the idea of completeness and readiness for battle. When his article appeared, the United States was nowhere near a state of preparedness and would not be so throughout the 1890s, including during the Spanish-American War. The biggest problems for Mahan and those who agreed with his diagnosis were skimpy federal funding and a tradition of no large standing armed forces in the United States. The latter was not as big a problem for the navy as it was for the army, but it was still a source of continuous friction between the executive and legislative branches of our government. There was also the decades-old debate, stemming from the days of Thomas Jefferson, about what kind of fleet the United States should have—one based on defensive principles and heavily dependent on commerce raiders and torpedo boats or one that was built using the latest technology available and focusing on the construction of battleships and cruisers. Critical to the debates was the issue of how much reliance could be placed on coastal defenses. Advanced planning and preparations were essential before any conflict. As Mahan was quick to point out, "There will be no time for preparation after war begins."

The navy, like the army, faced difficulties with bureaucratic infighting and persuading its officer corps to accept modernization. In the 1870s and 1880s, the navy had a number of "old tars" on active duty, and these older fleet officers acted as if navies still fought in the same manner as Nelson or Farragut. The important questions about modernization and the acceptance of new tactics, these holdovers from the Civil War era, raised objections and managed to stymie most proposed changes.

In 1873, a group of fifteen of the more progressive officers in the navy founded the United States Naval Institute as an organization of professionals that would provide forums for discussion on vital topics that had a direct bearing on naval operations. They also created a journal to spread ideas on how a modern navy should be equipped and to advance new theories of tactics and strategies. In addition, the institute provided history courses that stressed the evolution of naval warfare and how advances in technology had changed the tactics of naval warfare through the years. One of the prime movers of this was Commodore Foxhall A. Parker Jr., now long forgotten except by Civil War naval historians. Parker served as the commander of the Potomac Flotilla during the Civil War and, when the war was over, published articles and books on naval history. Parker's influence did not come through his writings but from his pull on his friend and colleague Captain (later Rear Admiral) Stephen Luce.

Luce, himself an author on naval tactics and history, was fascinated by the study of naval history and was especially intrigued by the way naval tactics changed to meet the introduction of new technology. The Naval Institute created a prize for the best essay submitted each year from the attendees. The first prize went to Commander Allan D. Brown for an essay advocating the abolition of distinctions between line and engineering officers in the navy. Honorable mention in the contest went to a young commander, Alfred Thayer Mahan, whose essay was published in *Proceedings*, the institute's monthly publication.

The Naval Institute's secretary, Professor James R. Soley, impressed with the quality of the submissions for the prize, stressed that future submissions

Admiral Stephen Luce was a major force in creating the Naval War College and led the call for a modern American navy. *Courtesy of the Florida Historical Society.*

Professor James Soley established a modern curriculum at the Naval War College and invited leading Americans to lecture on topics of interest. *Courtesy of the Florida Historical Society.*

Commander Alfred Thayer Mahan was the leading naval thinker of the late 1800s. His ideas on naval armaments and organization were adopted by the major navies of the world. *Courtesy of the Florida Historical Society.*

needed to be based on solid research, in turn based on relevant documents. Soley also declared that future essays should be tied to the idea that the navy was the first line of defense for the United States and, as such, was the premier American military organization. In addition, Soley encouraged institute members to research and write naval history with an eye toward developing tactics and persuading navy leaders to become more amenable to technological changes. Soley, working with Captain John G. Walker, chief of the Bureau of Navigation, one of the most important divisions in the naval hierarchy, began the task of trying to establish a naval archive, which did not exist at the time. One cannot do sound research without an archive and archivists to locate the materials needed in a timely manner.

In 1884, after much discussion and lobbying in Congress, the appropriation was made to create the Navy's Office of Library and War Records, with Soley as its first head. Soley then persuaded Charles A. Scribner and Sons, a major book-publishing firm, to commission a three-volume history of the navy in the Civil War. Soley authored the first volume of the series, *The Blockade and the Cruisers*; Rear Admiral Daniel Ammen wrote the second, *The Atlantic Coast*; and the young Commander Mahan produced the third, *The Gulf and Inland Waters*. It was Mahan's first book and was an important contribution to the body of naval literature. Research for his manuscript gave him the opportunity to look closely at the sea routes, possible bases and depots and potential problems that would be of interest to a navy attempting to control the Gulf of Mexico. His research also formed the basis for an article for *Harper's Magazine*, "The Strategic Features of the Gulf of Mexico and the Caribbean Sea," published in October 1897. The maps that accompanied this article clearly showed the strategic importance of Cuba in controlling access to a proposed canal across Panama. He stressed the dangers that could arise if a hostile power ever controlled Cuba and wished to harm United States commerce in the Gulf of Mexico. He also showed the importance of Key West to the success or failure of a U.S. blockade of the Gulf.

The decades immediately following the Civil War were years of rapid technological development in naval warfare. The development of dependable steam engines and electrical engineering had a tremendous impact on the

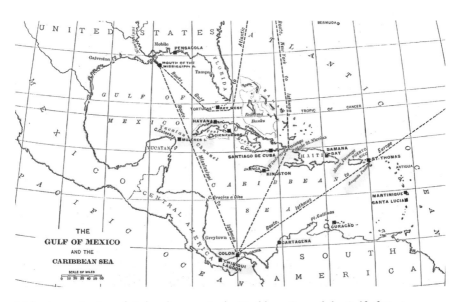

Mahan's examination of vital trade routes in the Caribbean Sea and the Gulf of Mexico showed how important Florida was in protecting the interests of the United States in the region. Harper's New Monthly Magazine, *October 1897.*

creation of more powerful and more efficient battleships. Improvements to the screw propeller ended the age of sail-powered warships, and individuals who still proposed combining sail and steam on the same boat were dismissed as relics who were simply out of touch with reality. The rifled gun, which produced greater destruction at longer ranges, rendered most coastal defenses obsolete, while the use of iron and steel in ship construction provided better protection against both ship-born weapons and coastal artillery. The introduction of new materials meant new designs, and the construction of stronger, faster ships touched off a corresponding round of development of technologies to defeat them. Gradually, the influence of the "new" breed of officers became the dominant force in the United States Navy, and the power of the "relics" diminished. John B. Hattendorf described the powerful navy that emerged: "If one can say that there is an American way of warfare, it can be found in America's reliance on technology and the application of new inventions to practical ends."

Innovation and the adoption of new theories of warfare became the operative culture at the Naval War College when Stephen Luce took over the reins of that institution. War, as he noted, was not the time for experimentation, and naval officers had to acquire a broad base of knowledge. Courses in naval history, tactics and logistics were added to the curriculum, taught by a faculty of active service officers who preached the doctrine of professionalism in every aspect of naval service. Students used "war gaming" to demonstrate their proficiency in applying classroom lessons to real life problems. Luce clearly understood that there was a difference between a scholar and a decisive leader and that both could benefit through the constant interchange of ideas. Leaders sometimes made decisions without properly evaluating alternatives, and Luce hoped to provide an educational foundation sufficient to make them stop, consider all the pertinent facts and not rush into a rash decision because of a hunch. Ironically, many of the new concepts Luce sought to instill were taken from some of his conversations about the education of military officers with West Pointer Emory Upton. Upton, in turn, had learned something about knowledge-based decision-making processes while studying the fundamentals of military education as taught in German military academies. The idea that warfare could be taught and learned was something new to naval theoreticians, most of whom held to the old concepts of instinct and upbringing as the major source of military leadership. "Military science" as a new study was just that—new!

Luce knew exactly who he wanted to be in charge of the Naval War College: his old colleague and executive officer on the *Macedonian*, Alfred Mahan. Luce's friendship with Senator Nelson Aldrich of Rhode Island had proved to be critical to the establishment of the college, but it still was not an easy task to persuade Congress and the navy brass to spend scarce funds for educating officers. Bureaucratic infighting almost scrapped the project when there were not enough funds left in the allocation to pay for coal to heat the building in which it was housed. Luckily, Mahan and his staff were able to sell scrap from a recent construction project to pay the bill. The lectures offered by Mahan were of a general nature in the first year of the college's operation and given by an array of talent, including Theodore Roosevelt, who lectured on the War of 1812. Mahan taught a course on naval strategy, and J.F. Meigs discussed naval gunnery. C.H. Stockton lectured on the strategic features of the West Coast, the proposed Isthmian Canal and the Caribbean Basin. Tasker Bliss was a regular lecturer on military strategy, while James Soley taught a course on international law and its relationship to naval operations. The courses were taught in an informal manner, and participation in war games and library research was strictly voluntary. The philosophy of the faculty was to make learning interesting and practical, and what each student got out of the courses was proportional to the time and energy put into them.

In 1888, Admiral Luce began to shake up the navy establishment when he decided to make the North Atlantic Squadron a laboratory for the Naval War College. Until this point, the United States Navy had never held regular fleet exercises, and neither did the army conduct large-scale maneuvers. The admiral became known as the "Great Drill Master" and often forced vessels into difficult situations, where command was given to younger, less experienced officers who had to figure out how to get out of the jam. As naval historian Ronald Spector observed, "Luce now proposed that the War College plan the maneuvers of the Atlantic Fleet and use them as a laboratory to test its new strategic and tactical theories." The objective was to "make theoretical instruction and practical experience go hand in hand." However, Luce's proposals did not fit with those of the secretary of the navy, William Whitney, who squashed the proposal. Fleet exercises did not become a staple of navy training until after the Spanish-American War had ended.

The years preceding the war saw many raucous debates between proponents of a program to expand the number and quality of shore batteries and commerce-raiding vessels and those who supported programs to construct more heavy battleships. Whitney's ascent to the position of secretary of the navy meant a short-term victory for the advocates of increased shore defense systems and smaller cruisers. What Whitney did do, however, was revamp the service's procurement procedures and investigate irregularities—why did a steam-powered navy have enough canvas on hand to equip Lord Nelson's entire fleet or over $1 million worth of old, antiquated uniforms rotting in bins in navy warehouses?

Whitney created the Endicott Board, a study group that made recommendations to him and Congress on ways to improve the nation's coastal defenses. Following the lead of Commanders William T. Sampson and Caspar F. Goodrich, the Endicott Board did yeoman's service and made some very thoughtful, if expensive, recommendations in its 1889 report to Congress. Whitney's term as secretary coincided with the completion of a number of cruisers initiated by his predecessor in the office, and he approved expenditures to pay for thirty additional ships. Some of these vessels incorporated the latest American technology, including the equipping of the battleships *Maine* and *Texas* with the heaviest armament in U.S. naval history. The *Texas* carried two twelve-inch rifled gun batteries, and the *Maine* carried four ten-inch batteries. Whitney did not approve of Luce or the War College, and he harbored a special dislike of Mahan. Because of his animosity, the Naval War College soon lost its old quarters and was transferred to Goat Island, home to the Torpedo Development Station, and placed under the command of Commander Caspar Goodrich. Goodrich approved of the college and its mission, and he helped it survive during the remainder of Whitney's term.

President Benjamin Harrison took office in 1889 and appointed Benjamin F. Tracy as the new secretary of the navy. Tracy, who is credited with bringing the U.S. Navy nearly into the twentieth century, immediately sought the advice

Modern navy ships, like the *Massachusetts*, placed the United States on par with most other navies in the 1890s. Mclure's Magazine.

of Alfred Mahan on how he could improve the navy. Backed by the president, he made a persuasive case to Congress for the construction of a modern naval force, with a core of twenty modern battleships and the capacity to be the nation's first line of defense. At the same time, he endorsed the Endicott Report on Coastal Defense. Tracy realized that the United States had to have a two-ocean navy because the journey around the tip of South America could take months. In order for the United States to have the ability to respond to crises along both its coasts, he proposed assigning twelve battleships to an Atlantic Fleet and the remaining eight to duty along the Pacific coast. Both fleets would be maintained in readiness at all times, for, as he stated, "a war, though defensive in principle, may be conducted most effectively by being offensive in its operations." These words echoed the ideas of Alfred T. Mahan.

With Tracy's proposal to Congress, debate began in earnest. The leading opponent of the plan was former secretary of the navy, now senator from New Hampshire, William Chandler, who strongly favored the increased coastal defense and a harbor defense system that featured small, armored monitors. It was a stiff fight, and Tracy's plan was not approved in its entirety. In 1890, with the strong support of President Harrison and with Representative Charles Boutelle of Maine steering it through the maze of committees, Congress approved the construction of three "sea-going coast-line battleships." They were the *Indiana, Oregon* and *Massachusetts*, and each played an important role in the Spanish-American War.

Tracy also took steps to revitalize the Naval War College and to make Mahan its commandant. Tracy realized that the new ships under construction would need highly skilled men to operate them. The fastest and most efficient way to ensure that the navy had enough capable officers was to assign them to the Naval War College as students. Aware that a steam-powered navy would need coaling stations, he attempted to persuade Congress to fund the purchase of islands (or rentals of the same) as refueling depots. Only one station was approved by Congress, and that was at Pago Pago, in the American-administered portion of Samoa.

The secretary of the navy in the second Cleveland administration was Hilary A. Herbert, a native of Alabama and a former Confederate officer. During his congressional career, Herbert served three terms on the Naval Affairs Committee and was the most qualified individual in the Democratic Party to hold the post. He was originally an opponent of the battleship navy proposed by Tracy but soon changed his mind after seeing the May 1893 naval review in New York Bay. Rear Admiral Francis Ramsay, chief of the Bureau of Navigation, pressed him to abolish the War College, and Herbert initially agreed to do so. However, on his way to install the college's new president, Captain Henry C. Taylor, Herbert read Mahan's classic book *The Influence of Sea Power upon the French Revolution and Empire*, which made sense to him. He reversed his earlier decision and decided to keep the War College open.

Mahan was transferred to the command of the *Chicago*, despite the efforts of Senator Henry Cabot Lodge of Massachusetts and Theodore Roosevelt for him to remain as the head of the college. Secretary Herbert faced a difficult Congress, but growing concerns by some congressmen over the powerful navies being constructed by Germany and Japan gave him a bloc of supporters, who pushed for reforms. A scandal involving several producers of steel armor, particularly Carnegie, Phipps and Company, brought additional political pressure as opponents of the battleship navy used the scandals to try to gut the program of new construction.

Closer to the Florida homefront, the Cuban Revolution of 1895 produced new fears that the state was vulnerable to attack by Spanish naval vessels. The Cleveland administration became involved in a confrontation with Great Britain, which had occupied the city of Corinto, Nicaragua, because of an unpaid debt. In addition, Great Britain became embroiled in a dispute with Venezuela over the location of the boundary between that country and British

The *Texas* was one of the modern American ships that defeated the Spanish fleet of Admiral Cervera at Santiago Harbor. Mclure's Magazine.

Guiana. When Venezuela broke off diplomatic relations with Great Britain and appealed to the United States for protection, Cleveland's secretary of state, Richard Olney, broadened the definition of the Monroe Doctrine to include all of the Western Hemisphere as an American sphere of interest. Only the long history of British-American friendship averted a military confrontation, but the episodes focused new attention on the need for a large, modern American navy. Enforcement of the expanded Monroe Doctrine would depend on the navy, and Herbert took advantage of the situation to press home the idea that this would be possible only if Congress loosened its purse strings. He also sought out the advice of thinkers at the Naval War College on how the United States could effectively assert its claims to have the final say-so in the foreign affairs of all American nations.

By the spring of 1895, the Naval War College began to plan for the possibility of a war with Spain, not Great Britain, and finding winning solutions for this possibility was to be the institution's "special project" for the upcoming year. The basic problems for the planners to solve centered on three questions—how to quickly mobilize all available naval forces, how to come to a firm understanding of the capabilities of these forces and how to supply their logistical needs. The logistics problem was tackled first by the planners since the establishment of supply bases and figuring out the rate of consumption of supplies once the navy was committed to action would determine its effectiveness in battle. Within this larger problem, factors that needed to be considered were the type of campaign or campaigns to be waged, their locales, the situation of the enemy and the limitations of the national economic machine on the production of supplies. An overall strategic plan of the war had to be decided upon in advance to ensure that adequate supplies could be stockpiled in bases easily available to the fleet.

Throughout 1895 and 1896, planners considered several possible scenarios, including attacks on the Philippine Islands and the Spanish mainland ports of Cadiz and Balboa, but these proposals were scrapped. The possibilities of Great Britain and Japan taking advantage of war with Spain to increase their holdings in the Pacific or even working in cooperation to mount attacks on Hawaii and the western coast of the United States were considered and discounted. By the end of the Cleveland administration, no single plan had been agreed to or approved by the Navy Department or the incoming McKinley administration. In 1897, the new secretary of the navy, John D. Long, assembled a new planning group to develop an overall strategy for a war with Spain, but few new ideas were presented. The year ended with no concrete plan in place, but there was a consensus that the main battle fleet

The sinking of the U.S. battleship *Maine* was widely publicized in American newspapers and eventually became the basis for the United States declaring war on Spain. *Courtesy of Joe Knetsch.*

should be concentrated in the North Atlantic, ready to intercept any potential attacks on the American coasts, where, the planners correctly predicted, something approaching hysteria could emerge in case of war.

The Naval War College planners argued strongly against spreading the fleet or any of its armored ships along the coast to protect individual harbors since that would greatly dilute the power of the fleet and its ability to meet Spanish admiral Pascual Cervera y Topete's modern fleet of battleships and cruisers in open combat on the high seas. As 1898 approached, there was no unified plan in place, and the planning was cut short in early 1898 with the sinking of the battleship *Maine* in Havana Harbor. There was agreement, however, on the need to blockade Cuba and to carry out the destruction of the Spanish fleet guarding the island.

The navy swung into action quickly following the destruction of the *Maine*. Although the two decades before 1898 had seen years of infighting and disagreements, the slow progress made in upgrading the service now paid dividends. Almost all of the armored steam vessels ordered by Secretaries Whitney, Tracy and Herbert had been completed and armed. Reforms brought about by the armor scandal had made the procurement process more efficient, and the oversight of naval inspectors ensured that the quality of supplies received matched the specifications issued. All things wooden on American vessels had been removed and replaced by steel or iron machinery, thus reducing the vulnerability of the fleet to fires ignited by enemy shells. The fleet was nearly up to its authorized strength, and the professionalism engendered by the faculty of the War College dominated the ranks of officers.

Despite the increased readiness of the American fleet, there was some confusion in Washington as naval procurement administrators, now armed with a $50 million appropriation from Congress, hurried to place contracts for war materiel with domestic and foreign contractors. Earlier plans to ship vital supplies to Key West and the Dry Tortugas had been carried out, however, and these were in place, awaiting the arrival of the fleet. Key West was designated as the headquarters for the newly appointed Rear Admiral William Thomas Sampson, who had just finished serving on the board in charge of investigating the sinking of the *Maine* and who had replaced the ailing Admiral Montgomery Sicard as commander of the Atlantic Fleet.

Tourists in the 1930s take in the crumbling fortifications of Fort Taylor. *Courtesy of the Ada E. Parrish Postcard Collection.*

Because of the earlier failure of naval leaders to persuade Congress of the necessity of acquiring overseas coaling stations and supply bases, Key West and Fort Jefferson in the Dry Tortugas became the major supply bases for the fleet. Food, fresh water, coal and other materiel were stockpiled under Sicard, who was convinced that war with Spain was imminent. Captain Robley Evans, later a rear admiral, described Key West in late 1897 as a busy place as Sicard expanded the base by setting up more storage for coal and other materiel. In March 1898, after the loss of the *Maine*, Evans became concerned that the port was vulnerable to attack by Spanish torpedo boats known to be in Cuban waters. He felt that if the number of American torpedo boat destroyers and cruisers was not immediately increased at Key West, these Spanish ships could "seriously damage if not destroy our entire force in a single night." He took his concerns to Secretary Long and his assistant, Theodore Roosevelt, who heard him out and immediately ordered the purchase of a number of fast yachts and tugs to be sent to Key West.

At the same time, Evans was given command of the *Iowa*, one of the newest ships in the navy. Evans returned to Key West later that same day and, with the wholehearted cooperation of Admiral Sampson, began drilling and training his crew to ensure their proficiency in any attack or battle that might come. Sampson, Evans and the other commanders in the fleet conferred often and made a proposal to Secretary Long concerning a possible attack on Havana. Some of these men had recently been to Havana and were very knowledgeable about the defenses there. They were certain that the harbor could be taken. However, Secretary Long decided that a blockade would be a better solution to defeating the Spanish and certainly would be less costly in terms of ships and men. When the order finally came to take to the sea and impose the blockade, it took only four hours for the entire fleet to be on the move.

Although the Dry Tortugas was seriously considered as a naval base by Assistant Secretary of the Navy Theodore Roosevelt because the islands were closer to Cuban targets than Key West, the waters around the Dry Tortugas were too shallow to allow any of the larger American ships into harbor. Some of the smaller cruisers that passed near them actually ran aground, since naval charts used survey information from a century before. The success of the blockade did not depend on using these islands as a major base, since Key West and the deeper waters surrounding it proved adequate for the fleet.

Imposition of the blockade called for the creation of three lines of defense. The first line was to consist of smaller, faster American torpedo boats and armed yachts that would report any movements of the enemy's fleet and protect the larger American ships from attacks by the Spanish torpedo boats.

Spanish prisoners taken from Spanish ships in American waters were brought to Miami under guard. *Courtesy of Arva Parks McCabe.*

The second line would be made up of ships in the light cruiser class, such as the *Detroit* or the *Cincinnati*, which, if needed, could move quickly to the front line but normally would remain two or three miles farther out from the smaller craft. The final line would be the main battleships, which would operate at a distance, determined by Admiral Sampson, from the others. To protect the battleships and other vessels from quick detection, the American ships were painted the now familiar "battleship gray," and to clearly identify them as Unites States Navy, a broad black band—four feet wide on the battleships and two feet wide on smaller ships—was painted on the smokestacks.

The navy was ready for battle. All that was needed was a declaration of war; after that, it would be simply a matter of finding the enemy fleet, destroying it and tightening the blockade until Spain surrendered.

6

THE AMERICAN ARMY

Oh, you have been doing many things in this time that I have been absent;
you have done lots of things, some that are well worth remembering, too.
Now, we have fought a righteous war since I have been gone, and that is rare
in history—a righteous war is so rare that it is almost unknown in history;
but by the grace of that war we set Cuba free, and we joined her to those three
or four free nations that exist on this earth; and we started out to set those
poor Filipinos free too, and why, why, why that most righteous purpose of
ours has apparently miscarried I suppose I never shall know.
—Mark Twain (Samuel Clemens), 1900

The United States Army was also poorly prepared to fight a war with Spain or any other foreign power. In 1896, the army had only 2,169 officers and 24,869 enlisted men, a reduction from the 28,953 soldiers that filled its ranks in 1871. The entire force available for duty in a war with Spain was smaller than that used to fight the western Indians after the Civil War. There was no concept of rapid mobilization of troops except for the occasional idealist in the ranks who realized that somewhere down the road we might need a larger military. Despite the fact that proven battlefield commanders such as William T. Sherman, Phillip Sheridan and John Schofield, who were all commanding generals of the army, led the army in the same period, none of them gave much thought to planning for a war outside the territorial confines of the United States. These men were not incompetent, but the prevailing opinion was that planning for future wars was not the job of brilliant generals; they would only issue general orders to the line officers beneath them in the eight military divisions that made up the army. Furthermore, they never had direct control of the staff officers who controlled the various bureaus within the army and who reported directly to the secretary of war. With the frequent changes of administrations and secretaries of war, the staff officers operated their bureaus as little fiefdoms. No comprehensive planning could be done for an international conflict under such a system, and army commanders acknowledged that such wars would be naval conflicts. The army's role was viewed as an occupying force, not as a major fighting force.

Most of the army's fighting units were dispersed in over eighty different frontier posts and coastal units. From Puget Sound, to Yuma, Arizona; from St. Louis, Missouri, to Portland, Maine; and down the Atlantic coast to Key West, the army maintained small garrisons as defensive posts. There were no large concentrations of troops anywhere.

The army's system of promoting officers did not lend itself to the creation of a modern, dynamic force. Young officers might remain lieutenants for a decade or more, since advancing to a higher rank depended on the retirements or deaths of superior officers. Following such vacancies, the next ranking officer was promoted, and subordinates moved up accordingly. Politics and kinship, as always, played a role in some of the promotions. Major General Nelson A. Miles, who was named the commanding general of the army in 1895, was related to former commanding general William T. Sherman by marriage, and Sherman ensured his continued promotions.

Some commanders achieved their ranks only because of their longevity. Some of the "volunteer" generals of the Civil War were allowed to assume lower ranks and pursue military careers alongside those who graduated from West Point. The inclusion of such officers in leadership positions was a constant source of irritation for West Pointers, who considered themselves to be professionally trained soldiers. The separation of staff officers and line officers in the chain of command also created friction. The result was that the United States Army in the mid-1890s was an institution without visionary leadership and lacking the organizational competence to plan for future wars.

The War Department, in 1898, consisted of ten bureaus with separate functions. Only the offices of the adjutant general and the inspector general officially reported to the commanding general. Communications between Washington and the frontier posts were the domain of the adjutant general, while the inspector general was charged with inspecting these posts and making corrections in conditions when they were needed. The other eight bureau chiefs reported to the secretary of war and, just as they had since long before the Civil War, operated with a free hand.

The Medical Corps also functioned as a separate bureau and experienced great difficulties in recruiting and keeping trained personnel, since army pay

General Nelson Miles was the leader of the American army when war came in 1898. He eventually led the forces that conquered the Spanish possession of Puerto Rico. Pictorial History of the Spanish-American War *(1898)*.

was low and its equipment was usually substandard. The army frequently hired civilian physicians to cover its needs. Faced with difficulty in acquiring supplies and equipment from the various bureaus, civilian doctors were frustrated by this lack of a centralized system. During the Spanish-American War, volunteer doctors blamed the army's cumbersome supply system for causing a large number of deaths and the needless suffering of sick or wounded troops.

The appointment of Nelson Miles as commanding general in October 1895 did little to centralize the institution's chain of command. Miles did not relish the political maneuvering of his predecessors and continued the power struggles between the secretary of war and his office. Although Miles had many outstanding characteristics as a military man and was a force when commanding in the field, he failed to bargain effectively with the secretary of war. Time and time again—during the lead up to the war and even during the war—he made recommendations, many of which were quite sound, only to be overruled by the secretary of war, who more frequently listened to the Joint Military Board and the Naval Board.

There was no bureau in the army's table of organization responsible for general mobilization or the rapid buildup of the army. The constant tensions between Miles and Secretary of War Russell A. Alger precluded the creation of such a department, which made planning for that eventuality impossible. Indeed, as Marvin Kreidberg and Merton Henry declared in their classic *History of Military Mobilization in the United States Army, 1775–1945,* "During the two years of steadily mounting tensions between the United States and Spain, no practical plans were prepared for a possible mobilization."

When war came in 1898, Miles made one more recommendation to the secretary, and that was to concentrate the regular army troops into a single camp prior to embarking for Cuba. Miles wanted to give his commanders the opportunity to hold regimental- or corps-sized maneuvers in preparation for confronting the Spanish troops on the island. Instead of concentrating regular army units, the men were sent to four camps—Chickamauga, New Orleans, Mobile and Tampa. The cavalry and light artillery were sent to Chickamauga Battlefield, while the infantry regiments were assigned to the other campsites. Under such an arrangement, no combined training could take place, and the coordinated training of these units was ignored. The army, manning eighty or more posts prior to the 1898 war, had never conducted combined maneuvers where all units were represented. Indeed, the Spanish-American War provided the opportunity for the first time in years for members of the same regiments to meet and renew old acquaintances. Individual units, after years of fighting some of the best guerrilla fighters on the planet, were very capable, perhaps more so than any army in the world, but units larger than companies or battalions simply did not exist.

Because of the lack of combined-force training in the prewar years, smaller units learned to attack in squads or platoons. In confrontations between small army units and western Indians, commanders had developed the technique of using a system of staggered formations in which widely dispersed soldiers assaulted objectives without offering a single massed target. In the face of automatic weapons and more sophisticated weaponry, like the Mauser rifle, used by Spanish forces, this tactic proved to be an advantage and reduced the number of American casualties. After the war, Spanish officers noted that this approach surprised their soldiers, who expected more compact units to attack them.

American army commanders did not expect their troops to be the major forces in the actions against the Spanish, since the navy was expected to handle most of the actual fighting. They assumed the army would be used to reinforce Cuban revolutionaries under General Gomez and General Garcia, but large-scale operations by the army were not anticipated. Miles saw that the main task of the American army would be to assist the Cubans in defeating the Spanish forces on the island and in establishing an independent nation. This concept fit perfectly with the ideas of the Cuban leadership, which feared that the United States might take the place of Spain and not allow the Cubans the right to establish their own nation as they saw fit. No major ground action on the island was believed necessary by the army or naval planners, who assumed the destruction of the enemy fleet and the establishment of a blockade would probably force the Spanish to evacuate the island. As Graham Cosmas wrote in *An Army for Empire: The United States Army in the Spanish-American War*:

> *Miles and other American generals favored this approach because they feared the consequences of plunging large forces into the Cuban jungles, especially during the summer rainy season when the roads melted into quagmires and tropical fevers made the island deadly to foreign troops.*

The army's strategy was based on the perceived weaknesses of the Spanish forces in Cuba. Worn down by three years of incessant warfare, most of the Spanish army was tied down in coastal cities or stationed in central and western Cuba. They had been under siege for three years. Tropical diseases ran rampant among the Spanish soldiers and killed thousands of them, while thousands more were incapacitated. The caliber of Spanish troops was questionable since many of those recently sent to Cuba had little or no training. Lacking adequate supplies, their morale was low. Both sides of the struggle sought to destroy the capacity of the other to feed and shelter their soldiers, and food shortages were very common. American intelligence experts estimated that the Spanish army numbered nearly 200,000 men, but the number of effective troops was thought to be less than half that figure. Diseases, desertions and deaths in combat took a huge toll on troops. The condition of the Spanish army was offered as proof to American leaders that the climate of Cuba would kill more soldiers than direct combat. The relentless actions by the Cuban Revolutionary Army made the task of defeating the Spanish much easier for the American forces should they choose to land in force. Indeed, Gomez and Garcia maintained throughout their lives that the Cuban Revolutionary Army could have won the war without United States military action if it had been supplied with guns and medicines.

The lack of adequate staffing was a major problem for the American army. The years of limited funding by Congress kept the number of staff officers on duty to a minimum. At the beginning of the war, as volunteers and National Guard units reported for duty, the Subsistence Department had only twenty-two officers, including the commissary general of subsistence, to find sufficient foodstuffs for the thousands of new soldiers. The Quartermaster Corps, which had the task of supplying uniforms, armaments and transportation vehicles, had only fifty-seven officers in 1898. Additional manpower came when the commissary and the quartermaster sergeants in the regular army were pressed into service. To add to the problems faced by these two important departments was the fact that both were under new leadership. Just twelve days before the sinking of the *Maine*, Brigadier General Marshall I. Ludington, the last of the Civil War quartermasters, was promoted to quartermaster general. His counterpart at Commissary, Brigadier General Charles P. Eagan, was appointed to replace retiring commissary general William Nash on May 3, 1898. As Erna Risch has written, "Both the Subsistence and the Quartermaster's Departments were physically unprepared to satisfy such demands from the field and, as in past wars, had to make extensive use of inexperienced personnel." The lack of men knowledgeable about getting guns and food to the fighting forces was a problem that was not solved during the short duration of the war.

Congress, as the keeper of the government's purse, did little to help the army prepare for war and actually hindered its preparations by not adjusting the funding available to Ludington or Eagan. Laws on the books since the Civil War restricted each department's efficiency by not allowing any expenditure beyond its appropriations, even in the event of war. Since expenditures could not exceed appropriations, the departments could not enter into any contracts to procure needed materiel. Because the war started in the last quarter of the fiscal year, Ludington had only $2.5 million to spend on supplying equipment before the next appropriations were made in Congress. The small appropriations for the preceding five or so years meant that the Quartermaster's Department had few of the needed items in its reserve inventory. In its 1890 budget, Congress, always looking to cut spending, even went so far as to order the Quartermaster's Department to sell off "surplus wagons" and even the famed army mules. Inspector general of the army General Joseph C. Breckenridge vehemently opposed this shortsighted action to no avail.

Breckenridge also loudly protested the impossibility of training men under wartime conditions to organize the transportation systems needed to provide frontline support. Combining the shortages of mules and wagons with unskilled, untrained drivers augured for a disaster. Orders that had been placed with the largest supplier of wagons, the Studebaker Company, were

Inspector General Joseph Cabell Breckenridge, a nephew of Confederate general John C. Breckenridge, opposed the congressional call to sell off army mules and wagons in 1890 as a means of keeping military spending to a minimum. Pictorial History of the Spanish-American War *(1898)*.

canceled, and the company turned its attention to supplying the domestic market. When the army approached the firm in early 1898 with orders for new wagons, it was informed that the approved plans for army wagons had been scrapped and that it would take at least a year to retool its operations to supply the needed wagons. Faced with a shortage of mules, the army sent Major (later General) Thomas Cruz on a hunt for the best mules he could find in Kentucky and Arkansas. Of course, the costs for such beasts had risen rapidly with the new demands, effectively wiping out the supposed savings ordered by the frugal Congress in 1890.

Probably no department took more heat for its performance in the war than the Medical Department. Hampered by shortages of doctors, trained hospital staff and the general belief that men who could not perform well in drill or on the battlefield would properly serve as stretcher-bearers or hospital orderlies, medics were forced to make do with very little. At the end of the Civil War, the Ambulance Corps had been the best in the world, but it disappeared when the law creating it expired in 1866. There were only two commissioned officers in the Medical Department in 1888 and none at the outbreak of the war ten years later.

Like other departments, the medical corps suffered from a severe shortage of transports. Few army leaders understood the need for a dedicated medical logistics officer who could anticipate the needs of frontline surgeons and hospitals. Failure to put officers in place that could master the mechanics of the supply chain meant shortages of medical supplies when they were needed most. Hastily inducted volunteer physicians and contract doctors had great difficulties in negotiating a labyrinth of competing departments, complicated paperwork and staunchly defended bureaucratic boundaries. How to order drugs, ice and other medical supplies required skilled practitioners with an understanding of the maze that connected the various departments.

In 1898, the medical corps numbered just 791 persons, and this number was not increased by Congress even after the men under arms had risen from roughly 28,000 to 275,000. As historian Richard V.N. Ginn described, "A hastily assembled expeditionary force arrived off Santiago, Cuba, on 21 June with seventy-one medical officers and eighty-nine reporters, the former to experience many troubles, the latter to cause many." Adding to the woes of the department and its patients was the refusal of the chief surgeon in Cuba to allow female nurses to assist in the care of the sick and wounded for a few weeks at the beginning of the war. Not until Clara Barton notified General Shafter and President McKinley of the situation did it change, and the first female nurses were sent ashore to assist the beleaguered doctors. Proper sanitation in camps was a persistent problem, and even after Surgeon General George M. Sternberg issued his famous pamphlet about the need for policing the camps and maintaining sanitary conditions, outbreaks of typhoid fever continued.

The most pressing need of the army, at least in the eyes of Congress, was that of improving the nation's coastal defenses. When the $50 million bill for defense was passed, the navy got the lion's share, but within the army's small allocation, three-fifths of the money was reserved for expanded coastal defenses. Florida had already held an important national conference on coastal defense in Tampa in 1897, and it was attended by many of the most important men of the state and nation, including Henry Plant, Henry Flagler, General John Schofield and Governor William Bloxham. Although the state press did not cover the conference extensively, it did send a message to Washington that something had to be done to protect Florida's long and vulnerable coastline. Like every other seaboard state and many of the major cities, Florida cried out for protection from the then feared Spanish fleet. Senator William Stewart of Nevada, certainly not a state with considerable coastline, sponsored a paper in support of more monitors to defend places like Portland, Maine; San Francisco; and Staten Island.

The move for more monitors, essentially Civil War relics and useless in the face of truly modern gunnery, was pushed by some of the old navy hands who had opposed the move toward battleships. However, the real push was toward increasing the effectiveness of coastal fortifications, long the sphere of the Army Corps of Engineers and the artillery. In 1897, the harbor at Tampa Bay had no true modern defenses, and the only Florida ports that were well defended were Key West and Pensacola, which for years had received most of the military's funding for such improvements. As early as February 1896, Secretary of War Daniel Lamont, responding to a Senate inquiry, noted that a sum of $25,678,860 would be used by the War Department to shore up America's coastal defense system and implement the earlier recommendations of the 1886 Endicott Report. This was more than twice the army's share of the $50,000,000 bill, but Lamont informed Congress that the expenditures were only one-seventh of the amount needed to implement all the recommendations of the report and would be spent on upgrading the protection for only three of the ports considered to be critical to the defense of the nation. To carry out all the recommendations of the Endicott commission would take ten years of constant appropriations, totaling $82,000,000, to complete the system for eighteen ports, and only two—Pensacola and Key West—were in Florida.

Fernandina received money to upgrade Fort Clinch, an old Civil War fort, which was to be retrofitted for two fifteen-inch Rodman guns and an eight-inch rifled gun. Rodman guns were of Civil War vintage and were nearly useless against modern armor. Plans called for the laying of a minefield to protect the city's harbor, but this was not completed until November, months after the war was over. As soon as it was completed, the mines were exploded because they were no longer needed. St. Augustine, home to St. Francis Barracks, the headquarters of the state guard, received money to construct one temporary shore battery, which was completed and turned over to army troops.

The meager amount of $13,260 was all that was allotted for the defense of the entrance to the St. Johns River, the most important port on the eastern coast of Florida. To its credit, the Corps of Engineers spent the entire amount, although the construction of the emplacements for the two eight-inch rifled guns was greatly delayed by the "nonarrival of materials" and delays in building platform mounts for the guns. The guns were not mounted until January 1899, too late to be of any use during the war. The most successful venture on the St. Johns was the laying of the mines, and this was not without tragedy. Lieutenant William Harts was put in charge of the mine laying and wiring them into an electrical detonation system. He was assisted by J.J. O'Rourke and a Mr. Houston. Somehow the wires were connected without having the proper resistance to current, and when a fuse touched the battery wires, there was an explosion that obliterated the unfortunate Mr. Houston, killed O'Rourke and severely injured Harts.

City leaders in Miami also petitioned the Corps of Engineers for protection against a possible attack by the Spanish fleet. By April 1898, landowners William and Mary Brickell had agreed to allow a temporary battery to be constructed on their property. Construction of battery mounting four guns and a battery of two ten-inch and two eight-inch guns started on April 18. By April 29, the "fort" plans had been reduced, and the projected number of guns also changed. Fort Brickell, as the installation was called, was completed by May 13, but according to the *Miami Metropolis*, the gun carriages were not in position "owing to the delay in the arrival of the specially constructed platforms upon which they are to rest." In the end, only two heavy guns were mounted there and never fired, even in practice. They remained there until the end of the war, after which they were rapidly dismantled and shipped elsewhere. Although Henry Flagler had used the argument that the establishment of this fort would give ample protection to the new town from the boats of the Spanish navy, historian Arva Moore Parks McCabe observed, "Ironically, although recently deepened to twelve feet, the harbor was still too shallow to permit the type of warships envisioned by the frightened people."

Key West and Pensacola received the vast majority of the funding for coastal defense. This is not without justification; Key West had a long history as an active naval and military base, while Pensacola was the home port for the American fleet that cruised the Gulf of Mexico and the Caribbean. Pensacola was also the home of a naval yard, one of the oldest and most important in the southern states. Because of its importance, Pensacola Harbor was protected by three fortifications—Fort Pickens, Fort McRae and Fort Barrancas. With allocations from the $50 million bill, Pensacola received new weaponry, including six of the newly developed rapid-fire guns. Key West also received six of the guns and additional batteries for the newly renovated Fort Zachary Taylor. The rapid-fire guns were primarily meant to defend against small, fast craft, like the torpedo boats, and to serve as antipersonnel weapons. Each base received batteries of "disappearing guns," which were rifled cannon that used the recoil from firing as a means of lowering the gun from visibility behind enlarged parapets. Fort Zachary Taylor was also greatly altered by the removal of the third tier and giving the fortification a lower profile from the sea, thus making it harder to hit from a distance.

The defense of Tampa Bay was crucial to the war effort since it was the point of embarkation for army troops invading Cuba. As the closest port with a railroad connection, it was the logical choice for the army's point of embarkation. The selection of this port, however, was predicated on the assumption that the army's role would be limited to no more than seven thousand men, who would be used to resupply the Cuban Revolutionary Army from time to time. The citizens of Tampa had ample reasons for fearing an invasion in the early stages of the war, since the city was home to the largest number of Cubans in the state and they had been instrumental in funding the revolution. In early 1898, the Board of Engineers drew up elaborate plans for the defense of Tampa Bay. Three islands—Egmont Key, Mullet Key and Anna Maria Island, then called Palm Key—were to be fortified and armed with powerful weapons. Thirteen six-pounders, an antipersonnel weapon used to defend against a land attack, were to be used on the islands. Eight twelve-inch mortars were slated for installation on Mullet Key, while Egmont Key was to receive six rapid-fire sixteen-pounders, four ten-inch breech-loading rifles and seven six-inch guns, which were to be placed on each end of the island. Three groups of twenty-one mines each were laid in the waters between the islands. Colonel William Benyard of the Army Corps arrived in Tampa to take personal charge during the first phases of construction.

Water shortages, mosquitoes and loneliness plagued the garrisons of these islands, which could only be reached by boat. Most of the drinking water came from cisterns since wells produced water that was too brackish to drink. The corps experienced considerable difficulties in finding enough civilian boats to supply these isolated posts during the construction phase. It also had to deal with the scarcity of civilian workers to supplement the small cadre of army personnel building in the fortifications. The location of these islands made them important to the protection of the bay, but events quickly overtook the need for the installations contemplated for the bay's defense. Like most of the other installations in Florida, few were completed in time to be of any use during the actual time of the war.

Congressional reluctance to fund these installations in advance of an actual threat, poor communications and a weak transportation infrastructure, as well as a paucity of boats to ferry construction materials, contributed to what was essentially a well-intentioned but wasted effort. The one positive for Tampa's port was the dredging of the main ship channel to a depth of thirty feet, which could accommodate much larger oceangoing ships than had used the port before the war. The new deep-water channel significantly increased the city's trade after the war.

7

THE ARMY ARRIVES
IN FLORIDA

If I owned Hell and Miami, I'd rent out Miami and live in Hell!
—Anonymous American soldier, 1898

With the coming of the war, Florida became the center of national attention. At no time in its history had the state been the focus of so much interest, except during the long, drawn-out spectacle of the Seminole Wars—and then the image was very negative. The national perception of the Sunshine State, took a more positive turn now that it was the forward base of operations for the army, . Florida was chosen because it had harbors closer to Cuba than anywhere else and a population that was greatly in favor of Cuban independence but not annexation. Tampa was the closest major harbor to Havana, closer even than Mobile or New Orleans, the two other harbors with port facilities that could possibly handle an invasion fleet and troops. Tampa mayor M.E. Gillette persuaded Florida congressman Stephen M. Sparkman to lobby the military to make Tampa its first choice as a port of debarkation for troops going to Cuba. Henry Bradley Plant, owner of the Plant System railroads, added his voice to that of Sparkman's. He wrote to Secretary of War Russell Alger, giving him a number of arguments for choosing Tampa and suggesting how the harbor could be defended against a Spanish attack by installing batteries on Mullet and Egmont Keys. His lieutenant, Franklin Brown, personally offered the use of Plant's Port Tampa facilities to President McKinley. After considering other options, McKinley agreed to make Tampa the primary port for the operations of the army.

Brown met the first contingent of troops to arrive in Tampa and opened Tampa Bay Hotel to accommodate the staff. Other men, including James E.

The luxurious Tampa Bay Hotel, the lynchpin of Henry Plant's transportation and tourist empire, was selected as Shafter's headquarters after beating out competition from the cities of Miami and Jacksonville. *Courtesy of the Henry B. Plant Museum Archives.*

Ingraham of the Florida East Coast Railway, were also lobbying Washington for the use of other ports along the eastern coast, specifically St. Augustine and Miami. Unfortunately for the Flagler railroad, none of these eastern ports was large or deep enough to accommodate the American invasion fleet. Tampa was to be the choice, and on April 15, 1898, Adjutant General Henry Clarke Corbin ordered the first troops, seven regiments of infantry, to embark for Tampa while other units were sent to New Orleans, Mobile and Chickamauga.

The first contingent sent to the Sunshine State numbered approximately three thousand men under the command of Brigadier General James Wade. There were no existing barracks to house them, and sites had to be found for their encampments. Major J.W. Pope was sent ahead to choose sites. Pope, who had never been to Florida, had only a couple of days to select sites for the camps, and at first, his final choices seemed quite good. His first choice of Tampa Heights seemed to be a perfect site for a camp, since it was higher than most of the surrounding area and had plenty of shade and good drainage. The other sites were considerably less desirable, especially sites near Port Tampa, which had very poor drainage. The sites were chosen at the end of the dry season, and Pope had little knowledge of the rainy season in Tampa. With the army's initial plan to use a small invasion force to assist the Cuban revolutionaries and to perform reconnaissance in force missions, the Port Tampa facilities appeared to be adequate. However, the army quickly changed its plans and decided on the use of much larger invasion forces, which meant that other sites were needed.

With the official declaration of war on April 25, 1898, Congress authorized President McKinley to call up 125,000 volunteers, and within a month these men were mustered into service. Another 75,000 volunteers were called for on May 25, 1898, and the regular army was increased to 61,000 men. By August 1898, the army had increased its strength to 58,588 men, while 216,029 volunteers were mustered into service, bringing its total strength to 274,617 men. Early plans, which called for a small force, were changed to increase the size of the invading force to 70,000 troops. Soon, officers in the commissary general's office, the quartermaster general's office, the Ordnance Department and the Medical Department were in a rush to send sufficient supplies to Tampa, despite the fact that Tampa could not accommodate such large quantities of men and equipment in such a short time. Obviously other assembly points, with sufficient space to accommodate training programs, would be needed. Fernandina, Jacksonville, Lakeland, St. Augustine, Miami and other, smaller towns were selected to meet the army's needs.

The first troops in Tampa were given a warm welcome by the local population. Local businesses were greedy for the new business; restaurants were ready to serve soldiers—at least white soldiers—who ventured into town; and the general population was bursting with pride that their town had been chosen for this important mission. A reporter for the *Brooklyn Eagle* described the scene:

> *On they come. White legs, yellow legs and red legs are swarming into Tampa, and the little town is almost beside itself with war enthusiasm and local pride...Yes, the white stripes are infantry, the yellow stripes cavalry and the red stripes artillery. My, how the girls are enjoying themselves.*

He then noted that many Tampa residents were busy poking fun at Henry M. Flagler: "Guess old man Flagler is kicking himself now." The fact that Flagler sat on five of the boards of railroads in the Plant System and was a member of the board of directors of the Plant Investment Company did not dawn on the crowd. Later, Flagler, Joseph Parrott and James Ingraham succeeded in getting a camp at Miami and harbor defenses on the St. Johns River. The citizens of Tampa were ecstatic about the arrival of the army and welcomed the soldiers with gifts, parties and grand balls at the Tampa Bay Hotel.

Officers who were rich enough to rent quarters at the Tampa Bay Hotel went about their duties in the lap of luxury. *Courtesy of the Henry B. Plant Museum Archives.*

White soldiers occupied five campsites chosen by Major Pope at Port Tampa, Tampa Heights, DeSoto Park, Fort Brooke and West Tampa. African American troops settled into an area between Tampa and Ybor City known as "the Scrubs." All of these camps were huge tent cities, as Paul Camp noted:

With minimal latrine facilities and crude field kitchens, these temporary tent cities were intended to shelter the invasion force for the short time anticipated as necessary to assemble the army and set sail for Cuba. Instead, the departure was continually postponed for one reason or another, so the bored, frustrated troops had to live in hot, humid, unsanitary camps for seven long weeks.

Common soldiers, lower-ranking officers and noncoms occupied huge tent cities in encampments spread across Tampa Bay, Fernandina, Jacksonville, Lakeland, Palatka, St. Augustine and Miami. This encampment near Jacksonville is served by a railroad siding and probably belongs to troops in the Quartermaster Corps. *Courtesy of Arva Parks McCabe.*

Within a very short time, the population of the tent cities outnumbered the local population by nearly two to one.

With the arrival of the army came the usual cadre of camp followers: illegal purveyors of liquor, prostitutes, gambling dens and a host of other businesses designed to separate soldiers from their pay. Just as quickly came excursion trains carrying thousands of spectators who had to see, close up, America's army in action. Hordes of reporters also came to town. Used to being treated rather well in certain cities, they had to scramble for accommodations in the now overcrowded city of Tampa. Those lucky enough to have comfortable budgets, like Richard Harding Davis, managed to find accommodations at the Tampa Bay Hotel, allowing them to hobnob with the officers. Most, however, were forced to take cheaper lodgings in the city, although they could frequently be found at the Tampa Bay Hotel refreshment counter. The camp followers, spectators, curiosity seekers and reporters all demanded food and shelter, too, which made the prices of simple items rise beyond the limited financial resources of soldiers who wanted something other than army rations. These problems of overcrowding, inflation, tourists, the arrival of family members of officers and the influx of prostitutes plagued other

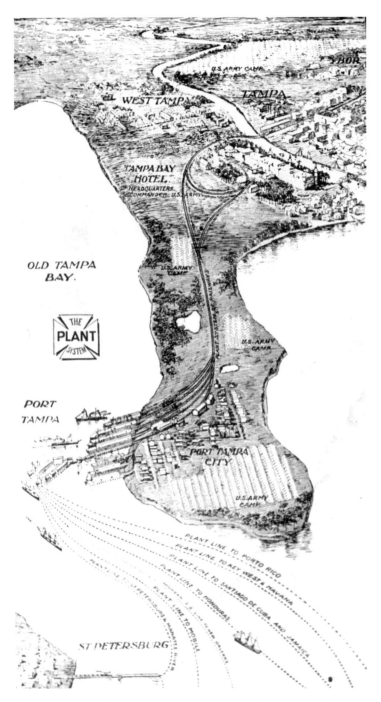

This map, produced by the Plant Railroad System, offered a view of the railroads servicing the port at Tampa. It also depicts several of the encampments around the city. *Courtesy of the Tampa Bay History Center.*

Mounted troopers pose before the grand Tampa Bay Hotel, which served as General Shafter's headquarters. *Courtesy of the Henry B. Plant Museum Archives.*

campsites but were nothing on the scale of those that affected Tampa at the beginning of the war.

When Brigadier General Wade established his headquarters at the Tampa Bay Hotel, he chose the most luxurious accommodations on the entire western coast of Florida. Although some reporters criticized his decision, there was no other facility available with enough room to accommodate the staff officers planning the invasion of Cuba. A small coterie of military observers, made up of officers from Great Britain, Germany, Italy and Russia, joined American officers at the hotel. One of the most vocal critics of the luxurious accommodations the staff enjoyed was a volunteer officer, Theodore Roosevelt, who just happened to stay in the very same facility at least three nights in the company of his wife, Edith, who had traveled from New York to be with her husband. Instead of roughing it with his troops, Roosevelt chose to live in the hotel.

Tampa's lack of rail facilities and an adequate port made the army's plan to use it as a centralized port of departure extremely difficult. Only two railroad lines serviced Tampa during this period, the Plant System and the Florida Central and Peninsular Railroad. The Plant System had the only connector

Above: Foreign countries sent military observers to witness the American buildup and later battles. Here the Russian attaché talks with his British counterpart. *Courtesy of the Henry B. Plant Museum Archives.*

Left: Although Theodore Roosevelt was only second in command of the Rough Riders (First U.S. Volunteer Cavalry) when the war started, he quickly became the most widely known personality of the war effort in Cuba. *Courtesy of the Henry B. Plant Museum Archives.*

Soldiers lounge on cargo after unloading their gear from the trains that brought them to Tampa. From here, they would find their way to their unit's area and erect camps. *Courtesy of the Tampa Bay History Center.*

line, a nine-mile-long, single-track spur, to Port Tampa. The Plant System's monopoly of the port facilities and the access to them created difficulties with army authorities. Soon, accusations of overcharges for shipping, the failure of the Plant System to double track the railroad to the port and attempts to block the traffic of its rival line filled correspondence between army authorities and Plant System officials. Freight traffic backed up almost immediately, and the slow delivery of needed military materiel infuriated the Quartermaster's Corps. Plant was accused of personally ensuring that excursion trains received priority scheduling over deliveries of military materiel. The situation came to a head when Adjutant General Corbin threatened to commandeer Plant's railroad as a matter of military necessity, forcing Plant to order his employees to give priority to military deliveries. Even then, his control of the Jacksonville Terminal Company made it difficult for competing lines to get their trains and cars transferred to routes leading to Tampa before those of the Plant System.

E.D. Lukenbill of the Florida Central and Peninsular Railroad, tried to interest the army in using Fernandina as an alternative camp at the beginning of the build up, but his letter to Secretary Alger was vague and did not specify that port specifically. Only later, after overcrowding and the spread of typhoid fever plagued the Jacksonville camp, was Fernandina used as an alternative camp.

The City of Tampa did everything in its limited power to make things easier and more enjoyable for the soldiers and visitors by expanding its infrastructure. When Major Pope was choosing the campsites, the city's engineer accompanied him to point out the advantages or disadvantages of a particular site. Soon, the electric company strung wires for street lighting to the areas where the regiments were encamped, the streetcar company began constructing lines outward to make it easier for the soldiers to get downtown and wooden sidewalks along the streets were rapidly constructed. In order to make walking and riding easier, Tampa paved roads to overcome the ankle-deep sand in the streets. The water system was rapidly expanded, and the lines were run to the various encampments. Meters were installed to regulate the amount and to allow the city to charge properly for usage. Overall, cooperation between the military and the officials of the City of Tampa was remarkable, and relations lacked the acrimony of the Plant System disputes.

Other cities followed the example of Tampa and provided what they could in the way of amenities for the troops. At Lakeland, the water supply was considered one of the best of the entire war and provided sufficient quantities to troops stationed in the city; the use of bathing facilities in the many lakes of the city was regulated, and time was set aside for use by soldiers.

The new city of Miami was soon overrun with soldiers, too. At first, the town was ignored as a possible site for an encampment, but soon, with pressure from Henry Flagler and James Ingraham, the army, against the advice of General Wade, decided to make it a model camp. The grounds for the proposed camp were cleared by Flagler's workers prior to the coming of the troops. Although he underestimated the size of the units sent there and the acreage needed for their activities, his efforts were much appreciated. Fort Brickell was quickly constructed, and the fort was to be armed with powerful enough guns to prevent any attack from torpedo boats or any other vessel that might try to enter Biscayne Bay through the main channel or the Norris Cut. A Miami home guard unit was created, and B.E. Hambleton was elected captain. By mid-May, the state government had sent enough arms to allow drilling to begin in earnest.

Nearby Coconut Grove, unwilling to be left out, also formed a militia under a Captain Haden. The army sent its first troops to the area at the end of June, mostly southern units from Texas, Louisiana and Alabama that were part of the First Division of the Seventh Corps headquartered in Jacksonville. Local historian Arva Parks McCabe described the city as "just not the place for 7,000 restless soldiers to live in tents in the middle of the summer. Even permanent residents used every excuse to leave Miami during the summer months."

Above: Local civilians frequently satisfied their curiosity about what the army was up to in its Florida camps by making all-day visits. Here a group of Miamians, dressed in their Sunday best, pays a call on troops stationed near Camp Brickell. *Courtesy Arva Parks McCabe.*

Right: Major General Fitzhugh Lee had served as the American consul in Havana before he returned to the United States to assume command of the Seventh Corps. He was just one of the ex-Confederate generals given commissions in 1898. *Courtesy of the Florida Historical Society.*

This simple camp near Jacksonville provided minimum shelter for these soldiers against the intense summer sunshine and torrential rains. Notice the clothing hanging on the line in the rear of the photograph. *Courtesy of Arva Parks McCabe.*

Camp life was difficult, and even dynamite could not loosen enough coral rock to construct latrines. Fresh water, sent to campsites in aboveground pipes, was too warm to drink. Soldiers bought cooler water from other sources and did not boil it, as required by the surgeon general of the army. The inevitable result was an increase in the rates of sickness among the troops. There were no facilities available for the soldiers to retreat from the heat or to find relief from the boredom that marked their stay in Miami. One anonymous soldier voiced the general displeasure of soldiers stationed in the city: "If I owned both Miami and Hell, I'd rent out Miami and live in Hell."

Jacksonville followed Tampa's example and provided adequate water, food and hospital facilities to the troops under the command of General Fitzhugh Lee, the nephew of Robert E. Lee and a former cavalry officer in the Confederate army. While he was in command of Camp Cuba Libre, troops were diligent in practicing good hygiene, especially in policing their encampments and covering their latrines daily. His successor placed less emphasis on these tasks, resulting in an increase in typhoid fever cases. Fernandina also provided water and well-shaded areas for the encampments to the east of the main town. Local women, in particular, took an active role in assisting sick soldiers in the hospital, often providing clean bedsheets and bedding. In almost every area of Florida, soldiers were welcomed and given whatever resources the community could provide. Many soldiers left Florida with favorable impressions of the people they met and the care they received.

8

IN CAMP

Gentlemen, you have now reached the last point. If any one of you doesn't mean business, let him say so now. An hour from now will be too late to back out. Once in, you've got to see it through. You've got to perform without flinching whatever duty is assigned you, regardless of the difficulty or the danger attending it. If it is garrison duty, you must attend to it. If it is meeting fever, you must be willing. If it is the closest kind of fighting, be anxious for it. You must know how to ride, how to shoot, how to live in the open. Absolute obedience to every command is your first lesson. No matter what comes, you mustn't squeal. Think it over—all of you. If any man wishes to withdraw, he will be gladly excused, for others are ready to take his place.
—Theodore Roosevelt to army recruits, 1898

The volunteer soldiers who made up the bulk of the army troops in Florida were a motley crew. Drawn from all walks of life and from every area of the United States, most of them had no experience with military life, and some had never even fired a weapon. The first task facing officers of the rapidly expanded army of 1898 was to teach the basics of being a soldier, including such tasks as organizing a campsite, recognition of rank, proper dressage, recognition of bugle calls and simple tactics—all of which had to be done before any training on how to load, fire and maintain weapons. Some units of state militia and National Guard troops were familiar with these requirements, although their training in annual camps and hometown drills had been sketchy at best. Growing from a core force of 26,000 men and officers in early 1898, the American army had reached 275,000 men by June of that same year. Whipping such a huge and inexperienced group of men into a

In an era before radio communications, soldiers relied on buglers to signal maneuvers, notify them of mess and pay call and lull them to sleep at night or wake them in the morning. *Courtesy of the Tampa Bay History Center.*

fighting force was a difficult job, but it had to be done if the United States was going to be able to defeat a Spanish army of 200,000 in Cuba.

Campsites for soldiers were often located on the poorest, least desirable land near assembly points. In Tampa, for example, camps were often established on vacant land offered to the army by local landowners or on city property. Much of this land flooded during the rainy season or drained poorly; some was little more than sand scrub or muck, home to venomous snakes, mosquitoes and other wild creatures. Camps had to be located within a reasonable distance of ports or railroads where a constant stream of supplies from army warehouses added to the problem of finding adequate space for all military activities.

Making camp, breaking camp or simply meeting the daily requirements of units for food and equipment meant relying on scores of wagons drawn by teams of mules, which required additional space for feedlots, blacksmith shops and wagon repair facilities. Cavalry units had to find space for corrals for their mounts, ideally two horses for each trooper. Vast open spaces, critical to practicing cavalry maneuvers or functioning as regimental drill fields, were at a premium, and in order to find suitable spaces, camps moved farther out of towns. Soldiers lived in proximity to their horses and mules, adding to the difficulties in controlling the spread of disease. Animal waste and human

Soldiers in a Tampa encampment play with a rattlesnake captured in the brush behind them. *Courtesy of the Tampa Bay History Center.*

The Spanish-American War was the last non-mechanized war the United States fought. Mules provided the brawn to move large quantities of supplies. In this photograph, mules pull wagons loaded with equipment, foodstuffs, tents and other materiel to docks in Jacksonville, where ships were waiting to take these Nebraska troops to Cuba. *Courtesy of the Florida Historical Society.*

Troops line up for review on a parade ground near Miami in this photograph. Notice the civilians—young children and women—in the foreground. *Courtesy of Arva Parks McCabe.*

Cavalry units were particularly hard-pressed to find enough vacant land for their unit tents and for feedlots for their horses. *Courtesy of the Tampa Bay History Center.*

A cavalry troop assembles for inspection at their camp in the Tampa Bay area. Notice the mule-drawn ambulance near the trees in the middle left portion of the photograph. *Courtesy of the Florida Historical Society.*

excreta provided excellent breeding grounds for the bacteria, parasites and flies that quickly produced staggering rates of sickness and death among the volunteer soldiers.

Daily life in camps was a constant round of learning how to march, erect and dismantle camps in the field and do the hundreds of small things that turned civilians into soldiers. Under the watchful eyes of officers, soldiers learned the accepted tactics of the day for infantry troops, such as forming skirmishing lines, firing rifles in squad formations and advancing as a unit in open areas. Under the hot Florida sun, infantry units practiced marksmanship and moving as a coordinated whole.

Cavalry troops spent hours practicing saber drills and training their mounts to hold steady in the face of enemy fire and the confusion of battle. Inexperienced officers also spent hours learning the most effective ways to deploy their men, becoming familiar with operating as a small cog in a larger war machine. The failure of army commanders to concentrate troops in larger-than-regimental-sized formations made effective training difficult, and the lack of large areas where troops of different units could conduct joint training also limited the cohesiveness of the American force.

Because many of the troops stationed in Florida before embarking for Cuba were raw recruits, officers spent a great deal of time teaching the rudiments of army maneuvers. Here recruits learn how to maintain a formation while "route stepping" over a considerable distance. *Courtesy of the Tampa Bay History Center.*

Nebraska soldiers are shown erecting tents in their encampment near Fernandina. *Courtesy of the Florida Historical Society.*

Although only a lieutenant colonel, Theodore Roosevelt became the darling of the American press, and his activities drew the attention of virtually every reporter. Here he is conferring with Captain Lee, a British army military attaché, during training maneuvers in Tampa. *Courtesy of the Henry B. Plant Museum Archives.*

Few officers had experience in leading troops because the few days spent in annual state militia camps before the war were occupied in parading before elected officials and local populations. There were some veterans of the Civil War who brought their experiences to the newly formed army, although most of them lacked the energy to properly supervise the younger troops or the knowledge of how modern rifles and cannons worked. Artillery units practiced assembling, aiming and firing their big guns in separate areas and received very little training in coordinating their fire with infantry and cavalry units operating nearby.

Life in the various camps throughout the Sunshine State was not all training and boring routine. Soldiers found time to visit one another in camp and to pamper camp mascots, usually stray dogs that wandered into bivouac areas and hung around because soldiers fed them and played with them. The science of photography had made significant strides forward, and photographers were always present at encampments, recording the training of troops and producing pictures of daily life to sell to soldiers, families of soldiers and newspapers. The American public had an insatiable appetite to become a part of this epic crusade, and photographs allowed them to do so, although many Americans took advantage of the excursion trains and came

Members of the Sixth U.S. Cavalry practice drilling with their sabers while stationed in the Tampa area. *Courtesy of the Tampa Historical Society.*

Troops of the Third Nebraska Volunteers practice marching on Pablo Beach (now Jacksonville Beach). The hard-packed sand provided an excellent surface for infantry troops and cavalry horses. *Courtesy of the Florida Historical Society.*

As soldiers do in every war, Spanish-American soldiers in Jacksonville soon adopted a dog of unknown origins as the camp mascot. *Courtesy of the Florida Historical Society.*

to see for themselves. The Ensminger brothers, who owned a commercial photographic studio in Ohio, sent photographers to the Sunshine State to record the military's activity. Individual soldiers purchased portraits to send home to families eagerly awaiting news from the camps. Not every photograph was serious in nature, and photographers knew that humorous photographs sold in the popular market.

Daily life did require soldiers to undertake a variety of housekeeping chores, such as policing the camps, doing laundry and maintaining personal hygiene. Clotheslines were strung from tree to tree, and the troops washed their uniforms in boiling kettles of water. There was no centrally operated laundry, and individual soldiers were responsible for washing their clothing. Communal kitchens under canvas shelters provided meals for the soldiers. The fare was not of five-star quality, but readily available sources of fresh vegetables, eggs and meat made meals edible. Once the army took the field in Cuba and relied on rations, thousands suffered a variety of gastrointestinal illnesses that took them out of action. Some resourceful soldiers earned extra money by providing services to their fellow troopers. The purchase of a barber's chair or an iron could become the basis of a small, but highly profitable, business.

Above: These soldiers stationed in Jacksonville pose for a group photograph beneath the Spanish moss and water oaks of Amelia Island. *Courtesy of the Florida Historical Society.*

Left: Private Alvin Lake had his photograph taken in Tampa to send home to his folks and to keep as a souvenir of his time in the army. *Courtesy of the Tampa Bay History Center.*

Right: A soldier with his full field pack and weapon carried approximately forty pounds. In combat situations, the pack was often tossed aside and retrieved when the fighting stopped. *Courtesy of Arva Park McCabe and William Straight.*

Below: Soldiers in the field endured harsh conditions. They were forced to utilize temporary facilities such as this outdoor kitchen erected near Jacksonville. *Courtesy of the Florida Historical Society.*

Soldiers stood in line with their mess kits when the bugler sounded mess call. One of the loudest complaints of soldiers in the Spanish-American War was having to eat "tinned" or "bully" beef in the field. Kitchen-cooked food was a welcomed exception. *Courtesy of the Tampa Bay History Center.*

Although much of the soldiers' time was spent in training for combat, there was plenty of free time to visit with friends and to take care of their normal day-to-day needs. Here a barber, complete with reclining barber's chair, lathers and shaves a soldier. *Courtesy of the Tampa Bay History Center.*

In Camp

Towns near army camps offered a variety of vices for soldiers. Gambling dens, whorehouses, saloons and other establishments flourished. There was little that army authorities or city leaders could do to control these activities, although Saturday mornings were filled with inspections and housekeeping chores that limited the amount of time soldiers could spend in town. Soldiers lined up to receive their monthly pay and, as soon as they could get permission from their officers, headed to see the sights. The purveyors of vice were waiting.

Military authorities did try to provide cultural and religious opportunities for soldiers in camp. Regimental bands frequently staged open-air concerts for the troops and for the crowds of visitors from the towns and cities nearby. Religious services, also held outdoors, were regular Sunday morning

These soldiers are ready for a Saturday morning inspection. Inspections like this were conducted regularly before the troops were released to go into town on passes. Notice the conical tents behind them. The American military was hard-pressed to supply the needs of soldiers and resorted to utilizing equipment, including woolen uniforms, from years past. *Courtesy of the Tampa Bay History Center.*

Infantry troops are lined up for a morning inspection in their battle dress. Inspections like these were held in order to ensure that all soldiers had all of their equipment and that the equipment was in proper working order. *Courtesy of the Tampa Bay History Center.*

A regimental band performs an outdoor concert for soldiers and guests from Tampa. Notice the umbrellas to the left of the picture. *Courtesy of the Tampa Bay History Center.*

happenings, and army chaplains reported a rush of conversions as the time for departing for combat in Cuba drew nearer. Chaplains in other wars fought by American troops have reported the same increasing interest in religion as combat approached.

Church services for soldiers were held in the open air. In this photograph, the regimental band plays hymns during Dedication Day at a Tampa camp. *Courtesy of the Tampa Bay History Center.*

Wives and family members of volunteer officers were frequent visitors to army camps. In this photograph, William Jennings Bryan, a lieutenant colonel in a Nebraska regiment, is visited by his wife at Camp Cuba Libre near Jacksonville. *Courtesy of the Tampa Bay History Center.*

Officers enjoyed a much better standard of living than ordinary soldiers did. Some were able to find quarters at Fort Brooke, a military installation left over from the Seminole Indian Wars and the Civil War. Some, particularly the wealthier officers, found lodgings at the Tampa Bay Hotel. If officers stayed in camp with their troops, they could count on having larger tents and the services of troopers assigned to perform housekeeping duties for them. Commanding officers of some volunteer regiments enjoyed the pleasure of having their wives visit them and stay in camp, a privilege that no noncom or private enjoyed.

All in all, American volunteer troops in Florida enjoyed their stay in the state, and many returned after the war as tourists or as permanent new residents.

9

SANITATION, SOLDIERS AND SCIENCE

The man was ill of typhoid fever, and his temperature was far above one hundred. When I reached his cot I nearly staggered with horror. The man's face was literally black with flies. His mouth, which was open—the poor fellow was too weak to close it—was filled with flies...In another case a man who died in the division hospital was found to be literally alive with maggots under his armpits, and his dying agonies were intensified by the movements of these vermin.
—New York Times, *August 10, 1898*

Only 345 soldiers lost their lives in combat during the Spanish-American War, but 2,565 died because of disease, primarily yellow fever, typhoid fever, malaria and dysentery. American troops in the Philippines had to deal with all these diseases but also faced additional danger from yaws, leprosy, filariasis, dengue fever, beriberi and cholera. The number of casualties in 1898 was small compared to the hundreds of thousands who died in combat or who fell victim to diseases in the Civil War, but that war lasted four years and saw millions of men take the field. The Spanish-American War lasted only a few months, and the number of troops involved did not exceed 300,000. Certainly, the institutional memory of the United States Army excluded what had been learned about the importance of sanitation and medical care in that great conflict.

The campsites chosen for the troops in Florida had many defects. Some, like those in Tampa, were situated on low, swampy ground, and many were next to tidal areas, where adequate drainage was impossible once the rainy summer season began. Others, like Miami, were high enough but suffered from sitting on top of coral rock, which made it nearly impossible to place "sinks" or latrines anywhere. Camps in Jacksonville suffered from the same problems, since they were usually located on open land that had been rejected by local residents as dangerous and unusable. The camp at Fernandina, on the other hand, was located on the sand dunes near Fort Clinch, which drained very well. This camp eventually became the major center of troops suffering from diseases they had contracted in other camps in the Sunshine State.

Poor drainage and poor sanitation produced ideal conditions for typhoid fever, while swampy land and tidal marshes were breeding places for the anopheles mosquitoes, which carried malaria and the deadlier yellow fever. The topography of Florida was not the sole contributing factor in the spread of diseases among the troops. Most were volunteers who took a rather cavalier approach toward orders from Surgeon General George Miller Sternberg, who issued detailed instructions on steps to be taken to ensure that camps were sanitary and free from disease. Career soldiers, on the other hand, accepted his instructions as another order to be followed; as a result, their camps were virtually disease free. Most of the troops stationed in Florida for extended periods were state volunteer units, like those of the Florida militia, which usually received poor performance ratings because of the uncleanliness of

Although small, the army's medical corps performed well during the war. In this photograph, ambulances are parked neatly beside a row of well-maintained hospital tents. *Courtesy of the Tampa Bay History Center.*

their annual encampments. Unfortunately, the comments made about Florida units were mirrored in evaluations of the state troops throughout the nation, and failure to correct the problems was a recipe for disaster.

At the beginning of the war, there was a consensus among medical men that yellow fever, the most feared killer of the day, arrived with passengers and foodstuffs on boats, especially boats from Havana. For almost two hundred years, this explanation of how outbreaks of the disease started in southern states was accepted by the medical profession as true. Typhoid fever did not come with mosquitoes as many believed. The real reason was that few soldiers dug proper latrines or covered fecal matter with lime. Despite Sternberg's order that all fecal matter had to be covered immediately, human waste was allowed to accumulate, and when a latrine became unusable, another was dug nearby.

In his study of the camp at Miami, Dr. William Strait detailed the army's original plans for waste disposal that called for trough systems that would collect the waste and wash it into an area where the tides would carry it into Biscayne Bay. Only soldiers camped near the bay built such a system, while those camped farther inland relied on shallow latrines or large tubs to collect the waste matter. Shallow latrines allowed the waste to be absorbed in the ground water and then floated to the top of the ground in heavy summer rains, where it collected in small pools. Typhoid passed from human to human, and the causative bacteria in the ground water passed through the skins of men who walked or waded through the pools. Using tubs proved to be just as unreliable, since soldiers assigned to emptying them often spilled them through careless handing. A third method, called a "floating privy," has never been clearly explained, and there is speculation that it was simply an enclosed latrine suspended over the bay or the Miami River, where fecal matter dropped directly into the water. Of the various methods of waste disposal used by the troops, none proved adequate. Outbreaks of typhoid fever killed some soldiers and left others sick and incapacitated.

When Sternberg created a board to study the impact of diseases on troop readiness in August 1898, he named three men to staff it—Walter Reed, major and surgeon, U.S. Army; Victor C. Vaughan, major and division surgeon, U.S. Volunteers; and Edward O. Shakespeare, major and brigade surgeon, U.S. Volunteers. When the Reed Typhoid Board, as it was called, questioned Major Daniel M. Appel, the medical officer at Fort Brickell, about the instances of typhoid fever in the Miami camp, he declared that most of the illnesses diagnosed by the board as typhoid fever were actually some other tropical fever, such as bilious fever, dengue fever or maybe even early stages of yellow fever. Appel was not the only army physician who questioned the number of typhoid fever cases among the troops, and nearly every camp visited by the commission found contract doctors, many from the northern states and unfamiliar with more tropical diseases, who simply refused to take typhoid fever seriously and blamed other fevers instead. The board estimated that these civilian physicians employed by the army correctly diagnosed only about half of the typhoid patients they examined. The board's preliminary report noted that typhoid was "covered up by many other names" and dismissed theories that suggested stand-alone causes, such as overcrowding, gastrointestinal disorders brought on by improper diets or the failure of northern troops to acclimate to the southern climate.

The failures of army doctors to diagnose this disease properly caused uncounted deaths and long-term symptoms among soldiers. When outbreaks continued for long periods in a particular camp, commanders simply ordered their troops to pack up and move to a new site. Some units moved several times, but the failure to take preventive sanitation measures and an ignorance of how typhoid was transmitted offered only short respites at the new sites. A similar lack of understanding of how the disease could be contracted contributed to the rapid spread of typhoid. Recovering patients who could transmit typhoid to other soldiers and civilians were often assigned to care for other patients in hospitals, and some were given kitchen duty until they recovered fully. Nurses—mostly men—and patients pressed into working in hospitals seldom washed their hands and continued to transmit the disease to other soldiers. Even clothing worn by infected patients was an important

Because of its location on the high sand dunes next to the Atlantic Ocean, Camp Fernandina had good drainage and was considered the healthiest army encampment in the Sunshine State. *Courtesy of the Amelia Island Museum of History.*

vector for transmission of typhoid fever, and so, too, were casual contacts between carriers and non-carriers.

There are no records indicating the use of female nurses at the Miami camp, but this was not unique. At Camp Fernandina, which became a designated collection hospital for the sick in Florida, the commanding physician forbade the use of female nurses. When Major W.N. Vilas made a request for female nurses to take care of the sick at the divisional hospital, Lieutenant Colonel L.M. Maus ordered him to withdraw the request. Even the famous Clara Barton and her Red Cross volunteers had difficulty breeching this barrier. At Fernandina, she noted in her history of the Red Cross, the organization could

Clara Barton, the famous Civil War nurse and founder of the American Red Cross, offered her skilled nurses for use in army hospitals. Some post surgeons were glad for her help, but others refused to allow Red Cross nurses in post hospitals. *Courtesy of the Florida Historical Society.*

not even supply ice to patients because of the refusal of Maus to allow female nurses in the hospital. "Had the chief-surgeon, Colonel Maus, not been so deeply prejudiced against female nurses in general, and Red Cross nurses in particular," she wrote, "we might have done a much greater work in the hospitals than was permitted to us." Instead of using trained female nurses capable of doing a proper job, Maus opted to use thirty-one army privates with no training or knowledge of medicine as nurses. These few male nurses were assisted by other equally untrained assignees from various units.

Not all army surgeons refused the help of trained female nurses. The Red Cross nurses found acceptance at Camp Thomas, near Chattanooga at the Civil War battle site of Chickamauga, where more men and women died than in all of the battles and deaths by disease in the Cuban and Puerto Rican campaigns combined. At camps in Jacksonville and in Key West, the Sisters of Mercy and Sisters of Charity nurses were permitted to assist in the care and feeding of the sick and nursed many back to health. Nursing patients with typhoid could be deadly, and scores of female nurses, along with their male counterparts, died from simply being exposed to the disease. The exposure of female nurses to typhoid at the Chickamauga hospital was studied by the Typhoid Board, and their deaths provided the basis of its findings on how the disease was transmitted.

Although there were no female nurses allowed in the hospital in Fernandina, local women did everything in their power to make the patients' stay as comfortable as possible. Cots, bedding and nightclothes were not available to sick troops when the army first arrived at the port city, but within a matter of days local women had organized and worked to provide bedding and needed clothing for the sick. Of all the hospitals in Florida, Camp Fernandina's was judged the healthiest, and much of the credit must go to the local assistance provided by the female volunteers.

Among the pernicious effects of typhoid fever epidemics in military camps in the United States during the period of May through September 1898 was the significant reduction of the fighting strength of many units stationed there. Almost 2,000 men (1,939) died because of typhoid fever, while the exact number of sick soldiers who were lost as fighting effectives was estimated to be in excess of 20,000. To investigate and report on the origin and spread of this disease, as well as many other related medical and sanitary matters, the Reed Typhoid Board visited every camp. Although its final report was not issued until after the war, the board correctly identified most of the ways in which the disease spread through encampments.

Finally, the board pointed out that all army surgeons, including the surgeon general, lacked the authority to enforce sanitary directives. Instead, they made

Medics of the Cuban Revolutionary Army worked closely with American medics to provide the best possible field medicine in the war. This group of Cuban medics cared for Cuban volunteers in training at Tampa camps. *Courtesy of the P.K. Yonge Library of Florida History, Gainesville.*

recommendations to field commanders, who then decided whether they would translate these recommendations into binding orders or simply ignore them.

Once American soldiers landed in Cuba and Puerto Rico, the number of epidemics of typhoid waned. Since most combat soldiers were constantly moving from objective to objective, their temporary encampments were abandoned before human waste and excreta reached critical masses. Although individual soldiers continued to contract the disease, instances of them doing so became fewer and fewer.

In the decade after the end of the war, Major General Grenville M. Dodge headed a presidential commission charged with evaluating the performance of American forces, analyzing the reasons for failures in certain areas and suggesting ways to modernize and improve the existing forces. Among the many areas that were scrutinized by the commission was the loss of men to typhoid. The Reed Typhoid Board report became the basis for the commission's recommendation on how to prevent such losses in future wars.

The Dodge Commission report became the guide for the reorganization of the army in 1903. The General Staff Act created a chief of staff and a general staff corps and placed line officers in control of the army departments. These new department heads would have the job for a maximum of four years, eventually producing a number of skilled administrators with real experience in evaluating the needs of the army. Most important for the medical corps was the establishment of a direct reporting link between the chief of staff and the surgeon general.

In 1908, Congress approved the creation of a reserve corps of physicians, scientists and surgeons that could be mobilized in times of war or as needed for disaster relief. With its new mandate for action, the Medical Department moved quickly to correct the Dodge Commission's findings that "there was not such investigation of the sanitary conditions of the army as is the first duty imposed upon the [medical] department by the regulations."

The tragedy of so many Spanish-American War soldiers succumbing to typhoid and other diseases provided the impetus for a modern army medical system—one that stressed sanitation and preventive medicine.

10

FLORIDIANS AND JIM CROW

The People's Party will settle the race question. First, by enacting the
Australian ballot system. Second, by offering to white and black a rallying
point which is free from the odium of former discords and strifes. Third,
by presenting a platform immensely beneficial to both races and injurious
to neither. Fourth, by making it to the interest of both races to act together
for the success of the platform. Fifth, by making it to the interest of the
colored man to have the same patriotic zeal for the welfare of the South
that whites possess.
—Thomas E. Watson, 1892

Although the agrarian uprising of the early 1890s focused on creating a
unified political party—the People's Party, based on economic status
rather than race—this movement had been thwarted by Democratic politicians
who waved the "Bloody Shirt" of the Lost Cause and who used the specter of
Negro domination to effectively abort these efforts. Throughout the Sunshine
State, relations between blacks and whites deteriorated as whites sacrificed
their chances for political power on the altar of racial hatred. Florida saw an
increase in the number of racial conflicts during the 1890s, from mini riots to
lynchings. The Jim Crow system dominated the state's social, economic and
political structures, just as it did in all the other southern states. Poor whites
squandered the opportunity to take control of their economic and political
destinies, while Democratic leaders took great comfort in knowing that the
issue of race could and did override any other considerations.

The major difficulties faced by blacks throughout the South found
additional emphasis in Florida. As noted previously, the economic difficulties

experienced by Florida because of the economic panic, the freezes and the increasing strains caused by the international situation meant that tensions were high and compromise was difficult. The violence experienced by blacks in Ocala, Westville, Key West, Wildwood and other localities would carry on into the twentieth century. Many Floridians feared competition from nearby Cuba if it should be freed or become a United States territory, since the "Jewel of the Caribbean" produced many similar products, especially sugar. Some believed that the growth of the chemical industry in Germany also threatened the phosphate industry, as seen in the increased production of European beet sugars. Many people saw the increased population of blacks in Florida as a threat to their own economic welfare and survival. As Davies and other sociologists have indicated over the years, the elements were in place for an increase in violence and mayhem.

Such was the climate that faced the famed Buffalo Soldiers when they arrived in the Sunshine State. Formerly stationed in remote frontier posts well away from white population centers, these Buffalo Soldiers had garnered a reputation for being good soldiers, dependable in battle and courageous individual fighters. Clinging to outmoded ideas, army officials moved these soldiers from the frontier and included them in the Cuban

Buffalo soldiers of the Ninth U.S. Cavalry, with their mounts, stand ready to board the *Alleghany*, part of the large invasion fleet of American ships bound for Santiago. *Courtesy of the Tampa Bay History Center.*

A Captain Bruce poses with his squad of Indian scouts at Tampa Bay. The scouts were attached to the Rough Riders. *Courtesy of the Tampa Bay History Center.*

invasion force because the army brass was certain that their African heritage made them immune to tropical diseases that might devastate white troops. Included with the African American soldiers was a small contingent of Indian scouts attached to the Rough Riders. Finding locations to station black troops in Florida was not an easy task. Wherever they were stationed, trouble followed.

The Tenth Cavalry, the last of four African American units to arrive in Florida, was forced to find a campsite in Lakeland while some three thousand men of the Ninth Cavalry and Twenty-fourth and Twenty-fifth Infantries filled camps near Tampa. Almost immediately, black troops encountered conflicts with the local white population. Writing home to his friends and family in Illinois, Trooper John E. Lewis observed:

> Here [Lakeland] *we struck the hotbed of rebels. Lakeland, Florida is a very beautiful little town, about 1,500 population and quite thickly settled by farmers or country people; surrounded by beautiful lakes, but, with all its beauty, it is a hell for the colored people who live here, and they live in dread at all times.*

Shortly after their arrival in Lakeland, black troops found themselves in a confrontation with Abe Collins, a white barber, that ended with Collins's death and the arrest of two black soldiers. Lewis described the events:

Some of our boys, after striking camp, went into a drug store and asked for some soda water. The druggist refused to sell to them, stating he didn't want their money, to go where they sold blacks drinks. That did not suit the boys and a few words were passed when Abe Collins came into the drug store and said: "You d----- niggers better get out of here and that d--- quick or I will kick you B---- S--- B------- out." And he went into his barbershop which was adjoining the drug store and got his pistols, returned to the drug store. Some of the boys saw him get the guns and when he came out of the shop they never gave him a chance to use them. There were five shots fired and each shot took effect.

In Tampa, conditions were no better, erupting in violence on the eve of embarkation for Cuba and sending nearly thirty soldiers to the hospital. An Ohio volunteer unit used a black child for target practice in Tampa, causing a riot that was put down only when someone called out a Georgia unit to quell the disturbance forcefully. The riot lasted through the night of June 6, 1898, and resulted in at least twenty-seven black soldiers and three white volunteers being so seriously wounded that they had to be transferred to a military hospital near Atlanta for treatment. Of course, the Florida press almost universally blamed the incident on the black soldiers.

As the war progressed, it became obvious that the prayer of the chaplain of the black Twenty-fifth Infantry that the war would help the blacks by demonstrating their patriotism and that there would be a "further clearing of the national atmosphere" was misplaced. According to Willard Gatewood, during their entire stay in Tampa and Lakeland, "the color line was rigidly maintained," despite the best efforts of white officers. Black and white regular army soldiers realized that they were comrades in arms, and on more than one occasion, whites who taunted or threatened black soldiers within hearing or sight of the regular army white soldiers stood a good chance of being severely chastised on the spot. However, the army brass decided that while in the South, they should do as southerners wanted, and the troops were segregated on the ships in the harbor when they left for Cuba.

The arrest of Sergeant Williams, an African American soldier of the Twenty-fifth Infantry in Key West, for carrying his gun in public gave Florida another black eye. The specter of a black soldier, ordered to duty in Key West and there to defend the citizens of this very exposed point, being taken into custody by the local white police for carrying his arms in public created a minor sensation in the black press. When his fellow troopers

African American soldiers led similar camp lives to those of their white counterparts, although they were usually assigned to less desirable bivouac areas. This African American barber goes about his chores in front of the tents of a black regiment. *Courtesy of the Tampa Bay History Center.*

freed him at the points of their bayonets, the *Richmond Planet* applauded the action with the observation:

> *This colored soldier is at Key West for the purpose of defending the lives and property of the citizens of Key West, Florida...We trust to see colored men assert their rights. If the government cannot protect its troops against insult and false imprisonment; let the troops decline to protect the government against insult and foreign invasion. It is a poor rule which does not work both ways. If colored men cannot live for their country, let white men die for it.*

In Miami, black construction workers employed by the Flagler railroad lived just a block or two away from the camp of white soldiers, and the temptation to harass these unfortunates was too much for the soldiers to resist. Instances of rowdyism were very common, and instances of random shooting at the homes of black workers were not unusual. The threat of severe violence breaking out was so great that nearly the entire black population of Miami fled to the safety of Coconut Grove. By the end of their stay in Miami, the troops and the local population were happy they were leaving, thus ending what Arva Parks McCabe has called the "Battle of Miami."

The constant insults hurled at blacks soldiers while in Florida and the violence they encountered soon led to a call from leaders of the nation's African American community for black troops to be led by black officers. Noting that the black press throughout the country was calling for this reform, the *Florida Evangelist* observed, "They are urging their race throughout America to refuse to enlist in the Army unless they are placed under Negro officers, and for once the black men of this country are a unit and are following their leaders." Later in the war, some black noncommissioned officers were given brevet officer's rank, although none above the rank of first lieutenant, but when the war ended, their commissions were revoked and the soldiers reduced to their previous ranks.

For black soldiers and the black press back home, the war brought home the stark reality of segregation and Jim Crow laws. Their hope was to change attitudes by showing the bravery and patriotism of black soldiers, but as time went on, they soon abandoned this line of thinking. The black press soon expressed the view that there was a real division between those who held onto the ideal and those who wondered if the black troops were nothing more than cannon fodder for their white leaders. The United States' expansion into the Philippines, Cuba and Hawaii, with their mixed-race populations, stirred some of the most strident debates. Why should black soldiers go and fight for the freedom of others when they were being murdered, tortured and denied those freedoms in their own homeland? Florida's Jim Crow laws and the attitudes of its white citizens did not make Florida a good base for black troops, but in this Florida was not different from most of the other southern states. Black units left Tampa in mid-June, "[g]lad to bid adieu to this section of the country" and hoping "to never have cause to visit Florida again."

Booker T. Washington, speaking before an audience of sixteen thousand persons at the Spanish-American War Peace Jubilee in Chicago, reminded Americans that the United States had won all of its battles but one:

> *The effort to conquer ourselves in the blotting out of racial prejudice...Until we thus conquer ourselves, I make no empty statement when I say that we shall have, especially in the Southern part of our country, a cancer gnawing at the heart of the Republic, that shall one day prove as dangerous as an attack from an army without or within.*

11

AMERICAN INTELLIGENCE
OPERATIONS

We can no longer afford to disregard international rivalries now that we ourselves have become a competitor in the world-wide struggle for trade.
—*U.S. State Department memorandum, 1898*

With over fifty thousand Cubans in Florida and many others with contacts and associates in the state, the problem of keeping American military activities secret from the Spanish was difficult. The Spanish government employed the Pinkerton Detective Agency to assist its already existing network of informants in ferreting out the plans and movements of the revolutionary committees and their sympathizers. The various Spanish consuls stationed throughout Florida and the rest of the South gave updated information constantly to the Spanish authorities, who passed it on to American officials charged with halting the filibustering and breaking up their operations. The publication of many of these communications by Consuelo Stebbins in *City of Intrigue, Nest of Revolution: A Documentary History of Key West in the Nineteenth Century* has opened up new areas of research into the shadow world of intrigue and suspense surrounding the outbreak of the Spanish-American War. Stebbins provides evidence showing just how sophisticated Spanish networks were. Florida's ports—Key West, Tampa, Jacksonville and Fernandina—became hotbeds of intrigue and espionage, and it is not surprising that the consuls maintained contact with a large number of informants who supplied information about filibustering expeditions leaving southern ports, and based on this information, many were prevented from reaching Cuba.

Spain had a long history of espionage operations, going back to the days of the Armada in the 1500s. American intelligence-gathering efforts, however,

Cuban Revolutionary Army (CRA) officers provided critical intelligence to American military authorities about the locations of Spanish troops, the terrain of landing sites in Cuba and the locations of CRA forces. They also vetted Hispanic volunteers. *Courtesy of the P.K. Yonge Library of Florida History, Gainesville.*

were merely "babes in the woods" compared to those of other nations. The first official American naval intelligence unit was created in early 1882 and was dubbed the Office of Naval Intelligence (ONI). ONI was placed under the Bureau of Navigation for administrative purposes and owed its creation to reformers within the naval establishment—men such as Admiral Stephen Luce, Captain French Chadwick, W.W. Kimball and Charles C. Rogers. The first chief of ONI was Lieutenant Theodorus B. Mason, a world traveler and a well-informed collector of data. With the support of Secretary of the Navy William E. Chandler and Commodore John Grimes Walker, the head of the bureau, Mason was able to avoid some of the usual infighting that often plagues bureaucratic life. Mason could not avoid all interference by other officers, but he had enough support from the secretary to develop and implement plans for gathering information from diverse sources, compiling it into usable forms and making it available to his superiors.

Captain French Chadwick, who took over in 1892, did not survive in the office long after the start of the second Cleveland administration, but he did manage to get the new secretary of the navy, Hilary Herbert, to send observers to Rio de Janeiro during the Brazilian rebellion. Later, ONI sent observers to the Sino-Japanese War (1894–95) to bring home information regarding the new power in the Far East. The Cleveland years were also years of economic depression, and the government cut back on its consular service, including the number of naval attachés assigned to the legations. Attachés were the main sources of foreign intelligence for ONI, which did not have an official role in the creation of war plans until the new administration of William McKinley. The appointment of Lieutenant Commander Richard Wainwright to head ONI, which became involved in the planning for future wars, greatly improved the office's stature. Wainwright was diligent in sharing the information ONI collected with McKinley's undersecretary of the navy, Theodore Roosevelt, and his friends Senator Henry Cabot Lodge and Commander Alfred T. Mahan.

Wainwright's major task was to develop information on Japanese plans in the Far East and on the Hawaiian revolution led by Sanford Dole and his Anglo-American colleagues. The islands had a mixed population, which included a large number of Japanese settlers. As a result, Japan was very interested in the future of the islands and American intentions. In an era of international expansion and competition for colonial possessions, knowledge of what Japanese leaders might do concerning Hawaii commanded the attention of the McKinley administration.

The rise of the new German nation and the creation of a modern navy under Admiral Alfred Von Terpitz signaled the entry of a large industrial power with an appetite for colonial expansion into the world's political arena. The United States needed reliable information about Germany's intentions. Elsewhere, disputes with Great Britain over the slaughter of seals in the Pacific Northwest, the boundary between British Guinea and Venezuela and British actions in Nicaragua made the likelihood of an Anglo-Saxon alliance between Great Britain and the United States more remote. What were Britain's intentions? Uprisings in Cuba and the Philippines absorbed the time and resources of ONI, which tried to piece together coherent possibilities of future actions by the Spanish government. French acquisitions of new colonies in North Africa and the Pacific, as well as the prospect of conquests in other areas, produced an array of questions concerning the future intentions of this European nation. Formulating proper responses to the actions of these nations required knowledge of the areas concerned and the size, strength and abilities of the nations involved. Wainwright's job was to gather reliable information for the new administration, which needed answers to these questions—and soon.

The latest Cuban revolution, begun in 1895, presented a volatile and dangerous situation just a few miles off the coast of Florida. Facing national bankruptcy but reluctant to lose this important remnant of its North

American empire, Spain poured men, money and material into the island in the hopes of quickly suppressing the rebellion. This did not happen. The Spanish debt, already higher than any in Europe, continued to rise, and credit was difficult to obtain from world bankers. As American filibusterers became involved, Spain desperately needed information about their activities and the activities of Cuban exiles in the United States. Although Spain could count on Spanish expatriates and pro-Spanish Cubans to provide some intelligence, these sources were not considered completely reliable. The solution for Spain was to hire the Pinkerton Detective Agency to monitor the activities of Cuban patriots and their allies, a solution that required tremendous outlays of cash.

ONI knew that Spanish resources were rapidly dwindling and would only get scarcer. ONI's network of naval attachés and American businessmen in Spain provided much of the information about the Spanish dilemma, but ONI also relied on networks of paid informants. By 1896, ONI was providing information to the Naval War College for use in planning for a potential war against Spain, and the agency began to prepare plans of its own for expanding its operation if war came. At the same time, ONI attempted to provide intelligence on other global hotspots, but after the sinking of the *Maine*, its attention was focused entirely on Spain.

The large number of Cubans living in the United States made gathering information about the island relatively easy. In addition, the large number of American businessmen with trading ties to the island provided another intelligence source about conditions on the island. Spanish authorities on the island were well aware of this, and their efforts to curtail led them to make numerous arrests. Individuals like Edward Atkinson, who had a number of active plantations in Cuba, were willing to share their information and added to the storehouse of knowledge available to ONI. The Plant Steamship Line, which ran boats between Tampa and Havana on a regularly scheduled basis, also became a major source of information for ONI. Some Cubans, who had immigrated to the United States earlier but went back to Cuba on business, were arrested for spying and were executed. The 1896 arrests of Mark (Marcos) E. Rodriguez, Luis Someillan y Azpeitia and Luis Someillan y Vidal created a sensation in American newspapers.

The newspapers of the 1890s were also important sources of information. Reporters roamed the island, writing detailed accounts of the activities of the Spanish army and including sensitive information about fortifications and the disposition of military formations. The American press, which had realized that Spanish attempts to quell the rebellion made great front-page stories and sold newspapers, was also a source of information about Spanish

These officers from the CRA were attached as advisors to American units and functioned as liaisons between American and Cuban forces when the war was underway. *Courtesy of the P.K. Yonge Library of Florida History, Gainesville.*

outrages against Cuban civilians. The well-publicized arrest of Evangelina Cisneros and the Arango affair, sensationalized in the press, brought national attention to the ineptitude of the Spanish colonial administration in dealing with the Cuban insurgency. Of course, the New York junta and its affiliated organizations in other cities were major sources for American intelligence, but the information they provided had to be carefully evaluated for truthfulness. Wainwright and his small staff had the difficult job of sorting through the vast amounts of information received, choosing the most pertinent data and placing the information into a proper context before passing it on.

From Madrid, Lieutenant Commander George L. Dyer, the naval attaché, reported on the attitudes of the Spanish people. In 1897, he reported that the Spanish people strongly supported their government's handling of Cuba and that persistent rumors of war with the United States were constantly in the newspapers. Dyer noted the high level of confidence the people had in the Spanish navy and their boasts about their navy's ability to beat American naval forces. Spain could bombard American cities at will, they proclaimed, and the United States would be helpless to prevent it.

From his German station, Albert Niblack reported the Spanish purchase of two heavy cruisers from the Italians; both were thought to be better armed than the *New York*, one of America's best ships at the time. Roosevelt asked the attachés and ONI to provide additional information on coaling stations available to Spanish ships, the firepower of Spanish vessels and the cruising ranges of the Spanish ships. With a small staff and a limited budget, ONI could not provide all the information Roosevelt wanted, but it did provide crucial information concerning the strengths and weaknesses of the Spanish navy, including the fact that many of the ships were not yet completed and some lacked crucial equipment, including batteries to turn the massive turrets of the battleships.

When the United States Army landed in Cuba, many of its officers had been briefed from a very thorough compilation known as "Military Notes on Cuba," the product of many years of research and intelligence gathering. Almost every officer headed to Cuba had a copy. It was prepared under the direction of Captain (later Brigadier General) George P. Scriven and was gathered from a wide variety of sources. It included maps of every major town, railroad schedules, the road system (or lack thereof), extensive notes on the topography and observations from personal reconnaissance. Scriven was assigned to the Signal Corps but had access to reports from attachés, consuls, American businessmen and travelers to the island. His most important source, however, was the information provided by the junta and its affiliates. Scriven started to compile the information in 1892, a full three years prior to the outbreak of the Cuban revolution.

A very large collection of maps was assembled by the Military Information Division (MID), a new organization created from the Reservations Division of the Miscellaneous Branch of the Office of the Adjutant General under the command of Major William J. Volkmar. Maps were placed on tables and crosschecked against one another to determine which ones were reliable and which were not. The maps came from a wide variety of sources, including the national archives of European countries (Spain included). Like the navy, the army soon had attachés assigned to overseas posts, and these proved to be valuable sources of more current information on the size and organization of various armies, weapons used by them and possible sources of supplies. These

Cuban veterans and civilians celebrate the American-Cuban victory over the Spanish at this 1899 celebration of Sand Key. *Courtesy of Mr. Cleve Powell.*

reports added much depth to the knowledge needed to prepare the United States Army for action in Cuba.

Unfortunately, just as the MID was making headway in amassing vital maps and information, the head of the Signal Corps, General Adolphus Greely, began a bitter battle to bring the organization under his command. Greeley believed that the Signal Corps had been assigned the duties of intelligence gathering, since a vaguely worded piece of 1890 legislation stated that the Signal Corps would "collect information for the Army by telegraph and otherwise." Greely's interpretation of this law was not upheld by then secretary of war Stephen Elkins or the commanding general of the army, John Schofield. By 1892, MID was assigned the responsibility for collecting intelligence via General Orders issued by Schofield. The same orders also made the MID responsible for making all military maps used by army and state troops. One final order made the MID responsible for all mobilization plans and for the transportation of all state troops "for the concentration of the military forces of the United States at the various strategic points on or near the frontiers of the country."

The MID quickly became a mini general staff, but without all the powers of such later organizations. The MID staff included eleven regular officers in its Washington headquarters, forty officers in the state militias and sixteen military attachés based overseas. Under the leadership of Major Arthur L. Wagner, this small staff attacked its assigned tasks with gusto and intelligence. One additional task assumed by the MID was the identification of foreign spies attempting to infiltrate units bound for the front or headed to Cuba. With the assistance of the Secret Service and the junta, the MID was able to indentify most of these individuals within a reasonable space of time.

Tampa and Key West were two key military posts for intelligence gathering in the United States. These two cities, with large Cuban populations that had contributed more money and other support than anywhere else, were frequented by members of the junta and the PRC. The many organizations that supported the revolutionary movement and the forty or more pro–Cuba Libre clubs in the cities presented Spanish spies with many opportunities for infiltration, and the Spanish were quick to make use of them. Spanish authorities considered Tampa to be "the very heart of the American conspiracy" and, as such, it offered chances to obtain vital intelligence on the revolutionaries and their American allies. Since the majority of funds used to purchase ammunition and supplies for filibusters came from Tampa and Key West, it seemed to be the most likely location for Spanish intelligence agents to ply their trade. Spanish agents were able to obtain nothing but the sketchiest information about the activities of the revolutionaries, and some of this was planted to mislead them. Even when Spanish consuls had accurate information regarding filibustering expeditions and pressured the American Revenue Service to stop them, they were often advised against pressing any legal charges because they could not win convictions in Florida courts.

Of the number of stories about the intelligence games played out in prewar Tampa, none is more famous than the "message in a cigar" story told by Tampa historian Tony Pizzo. The story, as related by Pizzo, was supposedly obtained from Cuban sources, but unfortunately it has proven to be just a myth. The crux of the story involved the smuggling of the *grito de Guerra*, or message to begin the revolution, allegedly wrapped in a cigar and carried to General Máximo Gómez y Báez, the commander of the Cuban revolutionary army. The plot included the bribing of Spanish customs officials at the docks in Havana with handmade cigars from Tampa. The one containing the message for the beginning of the revolution had a special wrapper that indicated to the courier which one he should keep for himself and pretend to smoke while in the company of the inspectors. Once the bribe had been passed, the courier went blandly on to complete his mission.

As Consuelo Stebbins has related, the message was simply too large to be wrapped in a cigar and carried by members of the Cuban Convention, a revolutionary cell in Key West. A chain of couriers including Gonzola de Quesada, Juan de Barrios and Manuel de la Cruz was used to get the message to General Gómez and his waiting forces. Although these men were all well known to Spanish officials and agents, their quick and stealthy journeys made the mission a success.

Another famous spy story, written in the dime-novel style of the day, is *Message to Garcia*, published by the popular Elbert Hubbard. In the Hubbard version of events, an American, Lieutenant Andrew Rowan, was dispatched on a dangerous mission to Cuban general Calixto Garcia, carrying the news that the United States invasion force was about ready to embark. Garcia was to give him vital intelligence about the disposition of Spanish forces to bring back to American commanders. The actual mission was less romantic than that depicted in Hubbard's novel, and Rowan was less than the daring figure of his imagination. Rowan, an old Cuban hand and the author of a book on the island, did risk capture, but he knew the location of Garcia's force, met with some of the general's men and quickly returned with the information. Most of the information provided by Garcia was not new to MID, but it did update some of MID's more important information about the size and dispositions of major Spanish forces. The story served to romanticize the roles of the revolutionaries and the daring young American officers who worked with them in support of the Cuban revolution.

After the declaration of war by the United States in 1898, American intelligence agents in Spain and Cuba monitored the movements of the Spanish fleet. No invasion was possible until this fleet had been rendered unable to harm the flotilla of ships carrying American troops to the island. Intelligence operatives in Europe reported that Admiral Cervera had left Spain with his ships and was headed to the Cape Verde Islands, but they were at a loss to pinpoint his destination after he left the islands. The news that the enemy's main fleet was out on the ocean at some unknown location was very scary to most inhabitants on the eastern coast of the United States. The fleet had to be found. Intelligence operatives searched for the fleet, telegraphing officials of every port that could accommodate the large number of ships, but nothing was heard about its location until it reached Curacao on May 14. Once this was known, American naval analysts could predict where it would arrive in Cuba.

With Admiral William T. Sampson enforcing an American blockade off the northern coast of Cuba, especially near Havana, the next most logical

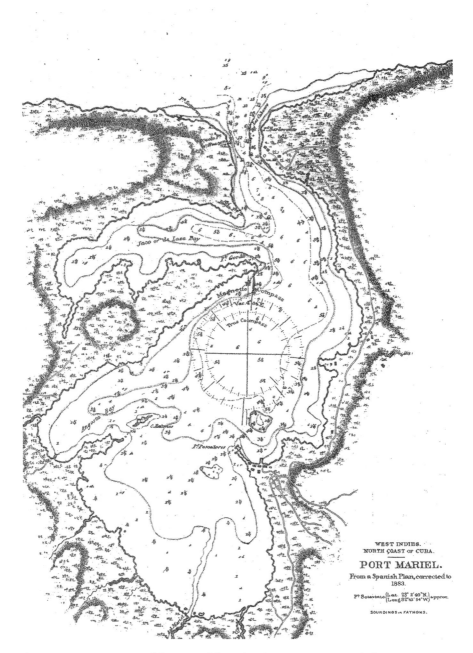

WEST INDIES.
NORTH COAST OF CUBA.

PORT MARIEL.

From a Spanish Plan, corrected to
1883.

P.ᵗ Sotavento {Lat. 23° 2' 40"N.} approx.
            {Long.82°43' 54"W}

SOUNDINGS IN FATHOMS.

Accurate maps were essential for successful naval and army operations in Cuba. Drawing on a variety of sources, including Cuban military officers attached to American forces, the Military Information Division (MID) provided up-to-date maps. *Military Notes on Cuba.*

location for a landing of Cervera's fleet would be Cienfuegos on the southern coast. Cienfuegos had good rail connections to Havana and a relatively deep port to handle the incoming vessels. Admiral William Scott Schley, leading a "Flying Squadron," was sent there to investigate and to blockade the harbor if necessary, but Cervera's fleet was not there. Five days went by before it was spotted in the harbor at Santiago, but another several days went by before this information led to a blockade of that harbor.

Much of the blame for this supposed intelligence failure can be placed on the rivalry between navy and army officers and a mutual distrust of each other's abilities, something that was to hamper cooperation between the services throughout the war. At the official declaration of war, President McKinley gave control of all telegraph cable lines coming into the United States to General Greely and the Signal Corps. The major lines serving Cuba arrived from Haiti and Key West, with a sideline to Punta Rassa, a small port at the mouth of the Caloosahatchee River. Captain James Allen, an energetic and highly competent officer, was assigned to Key West, where he quickly recruited Martin L. Hellings, head of the local Western Union office, as his assistant. With the agreement of his employers, Hellings was soon to be transferred, with the rank of captain, to the military.

Unknown to the Spanish officials, the Havana operator, Señor Villaril, was loyal to the revolution and quickly passed on whatever information he could gather without detection to Hellings in Key West. Villaril passed Hellings a message that Cervera's fleet had arrived in Santiago, not Cienfuegos, on May 19. Hellings immediately passed this vital information to the local naval commander, Commodore George C. Remey, and to General Greely in Washington.

As soon as he received the message, Greely went immediately to the White House, where President McKinley had set up a "war room." Greely assured McKinley that the information was correct and discussed it with the president and his advisors. Commodore Remey was asked to verify the contents of the message through Captain Allen's sources, which he immediately did.

When Admiral Sampson was apprised of the new information, he was skeptical, since Santiago made little strategic sense and Admiral Cervera was a highly regarded naval commander. After further confirmations came into the war room, Admiral Sampson sent a message to Admiral Schley to move his squadron to Santiago and to blockade the harbor. Schley did not believe the information at first and hesitated, concluding that there had been a mistake in transmission of the orders or that someone had given Washington false information to draw his squadron from the blockade of Cienfuegos.

Santiago was the first target for American forces. This map accurately depicts the city of Santiago and Spanish installations guarding the harbor and the city. *Military Notes on Cuba.*

These were not illogical conclusions, and Schley dallied in the waters around Cienfuegos for a number of days before moving toward Santiago, arriving on May 29. Only after he had sent a naval officer overland with Cuban scouts to verify the fact that the Spanish fleet was at anchor in the harbor at Santiago was he satisfied. Schley immediately established a blockade of the harbor, which effectively took the Spanish fleet out of action. The land invasion of Cuba could proceed.

Cervera's fleet remained at anchor in Santiago Harbor under the protection of Spanish gun batteries on shore. On July 3, after significant victories by invading American forces, Cervera was ordered to attempt a breakout but made a crucial mistake when he divided his ships into two small formations. After more than an hour's fighting, the American fleet destroyed all but one of Cervera's ships. The survivor, the new armored cruiser *Cristobal Colon*, fled along the coast and was ultimately run aground by the guns of the USS *Oregon*.

Remarkably, the American fleet lost no ships; only 1 American sailor was killed, and 10 others were wounded. In addition to losing all his ships in battle, Cervera also lost 323 sailors killed and 151 wounded. When the action was over, Admiral Cervera, 70 of his officers and 1,500 sailors were taken prisoner by the Americans. Unwilling to risk any more ships in battles against the American fleet, Spain abandoned its soldiers in Cuba. Without continued aid from the mother country, they were forced to surrender.

Naval and army intelligence operations against Spain proved successful, although these operations did not always go smoothly. Nevertheless, the creation of intelligence-gathering bureaus and departments in both services would prove essential in the long run to the American military in future wars.

12

PLANS, PLANS AND
MORE PLANS

*There had been about [five hundred] Spaniards at Daiquiri that
morning, but they had fled even before the ships began shelling. In
their place we found hundreds of Cuban insurgents, a crew of as utter
tatterdemalions as human eyes ever looked on, armed with every kind
of rifle in all stages of dilapidation. It was evident, at a glance, that they
would be no use in serious fighting.*
—*Theodore Roosevelt, 1899*

As troops arrived in Tampa, there was a change in command. General
Wade was replaced on April 29, 1898, by Brigadier General William
Rufus Shafter. In a conference between McKinley, Corbin and Miles, Shafter
was selected to lead the newly created Fifth Corps, the force designated for
the invasion of Cuba. General Miles was an ardent supporter of Shafter for
the position, noting that if someone who would not hesitate to get the job
done was needed, then Shafter was the best choice. Shafter was a gruff, no-
nonsense general of the old school. He was a large man, who weighed more
than three hundred pounds and whose bravery in the Civil War won him
the Congressional Medal of Honor. After the war, he took a regular army
commission and served in the Indian wars in western Texas as the lieutenant
colonel of the Twenty-fourth Infantry, one of the famed Buffalo Soldier units.
His best-known exploits in the West came from his extended pursuits of
Comanche, Mescalero and Lipan Apaches into Mexico. Under orders from
General E.O.C. Ord, who had begun his career as an officer in the Third
Seminole War in Florida, Shafter was quick to chase these raiders across
the Rio Grande into Mexico proper. With the aid of the highly competent

Left: General William Rufus Shafter (1835–1906), a Civil War Medal of Honor winner, was promoted to major general and placed in command of the U.S. Army Fifth Corps, one of two corps used in the invasion of Cuba. *Courtesy of the Henry B. Plant Museum Archives.*

Below: Henry Bradley Plant's palatial Tampa Bay Hotel was the headquarters of the American invasion force. This hotel was so large that rickshaws were used to carry guests through its maze of corridors. *Courtesy of the Henry B. Plant Museum Archives.*

Lieutenant John L. Bullis, he fought many small skirmishes with these Indians and angered the Mexican government in the process. When called to explain his actions, his testimony to a congressional investigating committee was blunt and to the point.

Shafter's no-nonsense approach to war won General Miles's admiration and led him to choose Shafter to lead the Fifth Corps. General Shafter was sixty-three years of age at the time of his selection, and he suffered infrequent attacks of gout. His large size made it difficult for him to get around at times. He was known to rely on his staff for information and ideas but did not shy away from giving directions when he felt they were needed. To smooth the transition to his new command and to pacify General Wade, both men were promoted to the rank of major general on the same day, eliminating any disputes about seniority that might have arisen.

It took Shafter three days to reach his new assignment, arriving late in the afternoon of May 2. Shafter set about planning for a reconnaissance force of five to seven thousand men when the army landed in Cuba. This force was to deliver arms, ammunition and medical supplies to the army of General Gómez. It was then to reboard the landing ships, sail to the northern coast of Cuba and deliver additional supplies to General Garcia. The original force tagged for this mission was five to seven regiments of infantry, one of mounted cavalry and "such artillery as I thought best." Shafter testified in front of the Dodge Commission that he did not contemplate taking much artillery, as he

General Shafter and his headquarters staff posed for this group photograph on the veranda of the Tampa Bay Hotel. *Courtesy of the Henry B. Plant Museum Archives.*

did not have the boats from which to land the pieces, and if they were landed they would have to remain.

Shafter received orders to cancel this operation when word came about the arrival of Admiral Pascual Cervera's fleet in Cuban waters. Immediately following the cancellation of the reconnaissance force, Shafter was ordered to prepare for an invasion of the port at Mariel, about twenty-six miles west of Havana. Once his forces landed and took the port, he was to entrench the area and await the arrival of the volunteer forces sent to relieve him. He would then take his regular army troops to conquer Havana. When Cervera's fleet was located in Santiago, General Shafter had to change his plans again. The capture of Mariel and Havana went by the wayside, and a new plan, requiring more transport ships and men, called for him to land his army either east or west of Santiago and to assist in capturing or driving Cervera's fleet out to sea, thereby securing Santiago. Within the space of just one month, Shafter had to organize three distinct plans, each with differing objectives and force requirements.

After much discussion between the naval commanders and army brass, Shafter was ordered to be prepared to launch the invasion in mid-May. The army regulars then in Mobile, New Orleans and Chickamauga were ordered to

Major General Fitzhugh Lee, the commander of the Seventh Corps stationed in Fernandina, also posed with his headquarters staff for this photograph prior to the invasion of Cuba. *Courtesy of the Florida Historical Society.*

Tampa immediately to reinforce Shafter's corps. To relieve the overcrowding at Tampa and get some of the troops closer to Cuba, Miles wired Shafter on May 10 to move as many of his infantry units that he could transport to Key West. Because the navy was not in position at Key West, Secretary Long asked for Shafter's departure to be delayed until May 16. In the meantime, Miles announced that he was sending regular troops down to Tampa and that, when they embarked on transports, he would take command of the expedition. The seriousness of his desire to do so was indicated by a remark by a congressman's wife, who noted that Miles had ordered new uniforms to wear in the field. Shafter, the nominal commanding officer of the invading force, was to get the troops ready to invade and then turn command over to his commanding officer. (Miles would eventually command the First Infantry Corps to capture Spain's colony of Puerto Rico.) Newly inducted, unseasoned and poorly trained volunteer units being sent down into an already overcrowded Tampa increased Shafter's difficulties in carrying out his new orders.

The problems inherent in incorporating volunteer units into invasion plans resulted in chaos and confusion. To make matters worse, the commissary

Ex-Confederate general Joseph Wheeler was one of the political generals given commissions in 1898. Wheeler is shown here with his son (left) and Colonel Leonard Wood (right). *Courtesy of the Amelia Island Museum of History.*

Major General Joe Wheeler (1836–1906) and his staff pose for a group photograph prior to their departure to Cuba. Wheeler, who was nominally second in command of the U.S. Fifth Corps, had been a Confederate general in the Civil War. At the Battle of Las Guasimas, the first major engagement of the war, Wheeler supposedly called out, "Let's go, boys! We've got the damn Yankees on the run again!" His critics blamed senility, but his supporters argued that he was simply overwhelmed by excitement. Lieutenant Colonel Theodore Roosevelt is at the extreme right of the photograph. *Courtesy of the Tampa Bay History Center.*

general ordered great quantities of supplies, mostly rations, to be sent to Tampa as soon as possible. No invoices or bills of lading accompanied the shipment of these supplies, and no one knew with certainty what was hidden in each boxcar. The quartermaster general issued similar orders for the shipment of tents, uniforms and bedding, and once more, vast quantities of material were sent southward without manifests or invoices.

To relieve the pressure of overcrowding and confusion in Tampa, Shafter and Miles discussed and ordered troops to be ready to board transports for Key West, but the lack of fresh water in Key West made stationing troops there, even on a temporary basis, impossible. Troops would require at least 100,000 gallons of water per day just for drinking and camp duties, and this water would have to be shipped by boat to Key West, an expensive proposition given the lack of transports available. Troops diverted to the Dry Tortugas would face the same predicament, since the only fresh water available there came from rainwater in catchments and cisterns. The need to boil cooking and drinking water required shipping large supplies of firewood. The problems of supplying water and wood and the difficulty in resupplying these essentials in the face of a possible enemy presence meant that Key West and the Dry Tortugas could not accommodate large numbers of soldiers. The only unit sent to Key West was the all-black Twenty-fifth Infantry, the second infantry unit of Buffalo Soldiers to encounter problems with whites on the mainland. Other than serving as a base for an army hospital facility and a place for rest and recreation, Key West did not figure in later army plans.

The rapid arrival of soldiers in Tampa soon exhausted the city's ability to accommodate them. Shafter had to order some of the volunteer units to Jacksonville, where he sent General Henry Ware Lawton to take command. Yet even as Shafter tried to limit the number of troops and alleviate the overcrowded situation in Tampa, additional troops were ordered to report to the city from Mobile and other stations.

An unidentified general and his staff pose in front of his headquarters tent. Americans, caught up in the excitement of preparing for war, wanted to preserve their adventures in photographs. *Courtesy of the Tampa Bay History Center.*

Shafter faced another major problem when loose talk about army plans made its way into the northern press. Admiral Montgomery Sicard wrote to Navy Secretary Long about a severe failure of security at both Tampa and Key West. He called for a tightening of security procedures at both bases and especially noted the need to detain the "press" boats from delivering news to their contacts. Censorship soon brought the ire of reporters, who complained bitterly. The movements of the fleet in and around Key West were of particular interest to the press, but censorship became so tight that no one was allowed to report on the comings and goings of the fleet or any vessel attached to it. Army censorship grew more stringent after reports of the voyage of the side-wheeler *Gussie* were published. This ship, which looked more like a river gambling boat than a gunrunner, left Tampa on May 10, 1898, to deliver weapons and other supplies to the army of General Gómez. So well known was the purpose of the voyage that both the *New York Herald* and the *London Times* published detailed stories about the progress of the ship, its cargo and its ultimate destination. The *Gussie* was scheduled to land at Mariel, but as it approached the shore, units of the Spanish cavalry, alerted to its destination by press report, were on hand to greet it. From beginning to end, the voyage was a fiasco brought about largely by the stories published in newspapers worldwide. The details of the voyage were so specific that Shafter ordered his aide, Lieutenant John Miley, to take over the telegraph station in Tampa and censor everything sent or received by reporters in the town. He was ordered to use the red pencil freely.

The policy of strict censorship of military matters continued until the army left for Cuba. When Captain John Brady replaced Miley on June 1, 1898, the *Chicago Tribune* quoted him as saying, "Anything relating in the slightest to the movement of troops doesn't go. I don't care if the Second Illinois is moved across the street, it can't be sent out." As the time of departure of the Fifth Corps came closer, security increased, especially after Lieutenant George Squire took over as censor. He made the cable companies issue the following statement:

The United States authorities declare that all messages containing information of prospective naval movements and current military operations are inimical to the United States and are consequently forbidden...If any such be found it will be stricken out by the censor.

In Pensacola and Fernandina, censorship was equally as stringent, and no information regarding military or commercial shipments was released for security reasons.

Before the age of radios or televisions, Americans followed the course of the fighting during the Spanish-American War with maps. This postwar map recorded the Cuban campaigns. Popular with the American public, publishing companies offered a complete set of maps. *Courtesy of the Florida Historical Society.*

General Shafter was always under the scrutiny of fellow officers, especially General Miles, and the national press. The constant change in plans emanating from Washington did not make the job any easier as each new plan diverted Shafter and his staff from concentrating on a final plan of assistance or conquest. General Miles's presence in Tampa during much of the preparations was distracting to Shafter, who recognized that at any moment, should he choose, Miles could take command of the entire force. The rush to launch an expedition put tremendous pressure on the regular army officers, and the inclusion of a large number of political appointees to staff volunteer units did not sit well with them.

The confusion at headquarters and at the docks in Port Tampa, therefore, was not the fault of any single individual but was endemic to an organization that had not been modernized since the end of the Civil War.

13

PORT TAMPA

Confusion on the Docks

Many of the officers...were young and inexperienced; army supplies from the North came down in immense quantities on two lines of railway and without proper invoices or bills of lading; it is often utterly impossible to ascertain in which, out of a hundred cars, certain articles of equipment or subsistence were to be found; and there was everywhere a lack of cool, trained, experienced supervision and direction.
—*Reporter George Kennan, 1898*

Tampa had been chosen as the primary staging area for the army because of its nearness to Cuba, but it had not been chosen for its excellent transport facilities. A lack of wagon transports increased the problems of loading and unloading supplies, and Tampa's dockworkers, who were normally numerous enough to handle the peacetime traffic in the port, demanded increased wages as calls for their labor grew.

An immediate problem that had to be addressed before troops began arriving was to find adequate storage facilities to house the supplies expected at any moment. Tampa was a small port in 1898 and was equipped with one quay, fifty feet wide in many places, and a few warehouses privately owned or leased from the Plant System. Little in the way of heavy equipment, needed to unload and load men and supplies, was available. With few resources available, the army had to improvise solutions on the fly. Temporary storage facilities to handle the numerous supplies sent to Tampa were built in record time, but they were off-site and up the railroad line from the docks. This meant that each shipment that came into the Port of Tampa had to be handled at least two, and often three, times before it was completely loaded onto the transports. This loading and transferring of materials took time and required skilled manpower that was in short supply.

The navy had, long before the war had been declared, made arrangements to assume control of most of the available shipping along the eastern seaboard and the Gulf. Army officers had to scramble to rent or borrow ships to transport their men to Cuba, a difficult task since ships that met the minimum requirement for such a job were in short supply. Once the ships were procured, the Quartermaster Corps had to convert them into troop-carrying vessels, fitted with toilets, kitchens, supplies of fresh water and sleeping quarters for the men. Ensuring adequate ventilation for troops below deck was also a major concern in the conversion process.

Captain James McKay of Tampa, a local shipper of cattle, came to the rescue and secured cattle boats for the job. McKay was given the job of assisting the Quartermaster Corps in converting these boats into troop transports and also helping army personnel in loading them in Tampa and unloading them once they arrived in Cuba. A few small boats from the Plant Line were pressed into use, but they were small vessels and were not designed to transport troops. With a shortage of skilled labor and few available materials to make conversions, the process was slower than the army brass expected, and the results were less than desirable. Ventilation systems that performed poorly, sleeping quarters that were very crowded and the lack of smaller boats to ferry men and materiel to and from the ships were major handicaps throughout the war as ships of all types were pressed into service.

An emergency appropriation passed by Congress assured the army of an additional $130 million for supplies, and the Quartermaster Corps and the Commissary Department lost little time in securing contracts for clothing, supplies, rations, fresh beef and the other items needed to meet the demands of a rapidly growing force. While welcomed, the new appropriation came after mobilization, and workers at depots in St. Louis, Chicago, Boston, Philadelphia and Jeffersonville, Indiana, bought whatever they could. The depot in San Francisco procured almost every available scrap of clothing for uniforms that could be had on the West Coast to outfit the Manila expedition. The army abandoned its normal bid process—that often took several years to complete—and expedited the purchase of needed supplies from private venders.

Many volunteer units arrived in Tampa without their full equipment. Supplying and equipping the National Guard or state militias had not received a high funding priority from either the state or federal governments. Consequently, many units arrived completely unprepared for going to war.

General Nelson Miles wrote to Secretary of War Russell Alger that many of the volunteer units arrived in Tampa without such basic supplies as blankets and cooking utensils, with tents left over from the Civil War that were falling apart and few of the basic necessities to sustain themselves in camp. The Thirty-second Michigan Infantry, considered one of the best of the volunteer regiments, actually came to Tampa without any arms, while the units that did bring weapons were equipped with Springfields, left over from the Civil War, that fired black powder ammunition. While this weapon was very effective in combat in open areas, the smoke produced by the black powder weapon gave away the positions of the hidden shooters to the enemy. Spanish soldiers inflicted a heavy toll of casualties on the Second Massachusetts and Seventy-

When the order came to pack up and move to the transport ships in Port Tampa, breaking camp required hundreds of wagons and thousands of mules. *Courtesy of the Tampa Bay History Center.*

first New York regiments, simply because these volunteers carried these antiquated rifles. Regular army troops and the Rough Riders were equipped with the new Krag-Jorgensen Model 1896 rifle, a weapon produced at the Springfield Arsenal that used smokeless ammunition.

During this time, General Miles noted, more than three hundred unopened boxcars were on railroad sidings leading to Tampa, and no one could vouch for their contents. However, as frustrating as the situation was, he informed Alger that "every effort is being made to bring order out of confusion." He went on to promise that despite the problems, "this expedition will soon be ready to sail."

Reporter George Kennan has left one of the more evenhanded descriptions of the departure of the Fifth Corps from Tampa and the confusion he found on the docks. Kennan noted that the railroad companies blamed one another for the delays, the army blamed the railroads for not getting their troops and materials there in a timely manner and the naval authorities blamed the army for not being ready to embark when they were. He also observed that the Quartermaster Corps and the commissary officers were relatively new to their jobs, a result of allowing many veterans to transfer to the volunteer corps at higher ranks and, presumably, salaries. Given the depleted corps of regular

Soldiers prepare to board a transport ship in Tampa Harbor under the watchful eyes of African American stevedores. *Courtesy of the Tampa Bay History Center.*

officers, the lack of training of younger staff members and the necessity of relying on new recruits, volunteer quartermasters and commissary officers, it is a wonder that the expedition got off at all.

In his widely acclaimed *Rough Riders* and, later, in his autobiography, Theodore Roosevelt placed the blame for whatever he felt went wrong in the war on regular army officers, who bungled every job they were given. The confusion that reigned in Tampa had a single cause—an army filled with incompetent officers who spent their time ogling the girls in their new, pretty dresses from the veranda of the Tampa Bay Hotel. Roosevelt disdained the luxury of the hotel and claimed that he "spent very little time there." As his

Loaded with men and officers, the *Concho* casts off its mooring lines and heads to a rendezvous with other transport ships outside Tampa's harbor. *Courtesy of the Tampa Bay History Center.*

biographer, Edmund Morris, noted, this is not the truth of the matter. "Actually, he spent three nights in its luxurious accommodations, for Edith [his wife] came down to Tampa, and Colonel [Leonard] Wood discreetly allowed him leave from before dinner to after breakfast each day." This statement clearly contradicts Roosevelt's public statements. Edith was escorted to Tampa by famed reporter, and Roosevelt admirer, Richard Harding Davis, who was one of General Shafter's most vitriolic critics.

Roosevelt also described the rather desolate "pine covered sand flat," designated as the Rough Riders' camp, as covered in dust and with confusion all around; once the Rough Riders appeared on the scene, it was transformed into a model of order and efficiency. Once the volunteers arrived, organized drills, unit inspections, cleanliness in camps, improved sanitary conditions and general order prevailed. By choosing to glorify the actions of the volunteer units and to condemn the regular army, politician Roosevelt was caging votes.

Perhaps the most egregious example of Roosevelt's one-sided view of the incompetence of the regular army was his now infamous story of how the Rough Riders had to seize control of the *Yucatan*, a ship headed for Cuba. As he told it, the Rough Riders, fearful of missing the invasion of Cuba, commandeered a coal train headed to the Port of Tampa, jumping off the train when it stopped and rushing pell-mell to seize the *Yucatan* before a rival unit, the Seventy-first New York Volunteers, could board. According to Teddy, all of this occurred in the midst of tremendous confusion, with Roosevelt and Colonel Leonard Wood running frantically hither and yon looking for someone to give them directions to the ship. Wood, in his diary, also noted the confusion but declared that Brigadier General Charles Humphreys gave him the orders to board the *Yucatan*. He does not mention anything about the Seventy-first New York.

The story would have been accepted as definitive had it not been for the testimony of Captain James McKay, the person in charge of loading the ships. In testimony in front of the postwar Dodge Commission, McKay noted that there was some confusion because some ships were overcrowded, and transfers were needed to straighten out the problem. However, he had already submitted manifests for each unit, which contained the name of the ship and its number, painted in big black letters on the main smokestack and on the side below the name of the vessel. The First Volunteer Cavalry, the Rough Riders, were indeed supposed to be on the *Yucatan*, but there is no mention of the Seventy-first New York also being scheduled to board it.

Upon hearing of McKay's testimony, Roosevelt replied, reiterating his own earlier testimony about the confusion and echoing what he was later to write in his book. In reply to Roosevelt's second round of testimony, General Shafter submitted the letter he had received from Major Leon S. Roudiez, who oversaw that portion of the docks during the loading of the Rough Riders. Roudiez noted that Roosevelt approached the *Yucatan* with his troops, two abreast, and requested permission to board. Just as Roudiez was about to answer the request, Colonel Wood shouted down from the second deck, "This is it boys, come aboard!" Roosevelt asked again for permission to board, which Roudiez granted, and the unit marched up the gangplank two by two. Shafter's testimony and that of General Charles Humphreys supported Major Roudiez. It is interesting to note that in the many memoirs of the Rough Rider veterans, none considered the boarding of their vessel as a seizure, and none mentioned the Seventy-first New York. Not surprisingly, Roosevelt declared that he never saw Captain McKay, nor had he ever heard of him until he testified before the commission. Roosevelt's version is a story about the good-natured rivalry between volunteer units trying to board a ship amid confusion brought on by the incompetence of regular army officers in charge. This theme constantly appears in *Rough Riders* and is a political statement, not historical fact.

Captain James McKay came from a long line of shipping men who were famous for their long-established cattle trade with Cuba. He was the son of a famous Civil War blockade runner and ship owner, James McKay Sr. Although he maintained the family's trade with Cuba after the beginning of the revolution, he also used the small, fast *Fanita* to haul men and arms to the Revolutionary Army. In 1886, he threw in his lot with the Plant Steamship Company and was soon captaining the *Mascotte* and the *Olivette* to and from Cuba. He was twice elected to the state senate and for a time was the U.S. marshal for the Southern District of Florida. He also served a two-year term as mayor of Tampa. His knowledge of the coasts of Cuba and Tampa Bay, coupled with his long experience in loading and unloading vessels, was exactly what the army needed at the beginning of the war. Working under Colonel Charles Humphreys, he performed his task as well as could be expected in such trying circumstances.

In his testimony in front of the Dodge Commission, newly promoted Brigadier General Humphreys declared:

> He [McKay] *was my principal assistant. He came to me by order of the Secretary of War and was a most valuable man…He was an exceedingly level headed man. At Port Tampa, and subsequently in Cuba, his range of duties with ocean transportation were exceedingly*

great. He did everything an exceptionally good man could do in that very responsible position.

Without a large number of trained stevedores; with limited space on a narrow quay; lacking lighters to move men, water and supplies; and unmarked cars loaded with military supplies, the fact that McKay managed to get the expedition out at all is remarkable. Just how important was McKay to the final movement of the troops? According to General Shafter, every person in the loading operation knew that Captain McKay was in charge, and he was obeyed as if he were a ranking officer in the regular army. Interestingly, once again, none of Roosevelt's biographers have noted the role of Captain McKay, nor have they even cited the Dodge Commission testimony of McKay, Shafter, Humphreys or Roosevelt himself. And what set Roosevelt off about McKay's testimony? When asked by General James A. Beaver of the Pennsylvania Volunteers and member of the Dodge Commission about the Rough Riders' seizure of the *Yucatan*, McKay bluntly declared, "They didn't do anything of the kind."

The McKay testimony was not the only thing that irritated the future president about his experience in Tampa. The Rough Riders were not welcomed with the open arms he had come to expect when they reached the Tampa city limits. Indeed, Colonel Wood was asked by Mayor M.E. Gillette to prevent his troops from marching directly into town. This rather blunt request stemmed from the fact that other volunteer units had already created some difficulties in the town, and for many citizens, the Rough Riders were just another bunch of the same hooligans. Another reason was that their entry into Florida was anything but a pleasant experience for a number of Floridians, who witnessed the rather crude character of some of the men. Some merchants along their route had been "hoodwinked" by members of the unit, who stole goods and took them back to the train.

Roy Cashion wrote letters to his hometown newspaper that were later published posthumously. "The fourth day began at Tallahassee," wrote Roy, "so while the horse were taken out of the cars and fed which took five hours, us boys made up a foraging party." In a scene reminiscent of Jimmy Buffet's "Great Filling Station Holdup," Cashion continued:

Some of us would crowd around the storekeeper and tell him all about cowboy life while the rest of them did their duty in filling their blouses with everything good to eat...As we were going back to the car with our spoils we ran into Major Brodie. He gave us a sly wink and pretended to be awful mad. He said we hadn't ought to come where he could see us with stuff like that, as it was his duty to keep us from it. He said just so he didn't see us it was all right.

Rough Rider Theodore Miller wrote about the regiment's stopover in Tallahassee, where troopers raided the chicken coops and hog pens of local residents. "Our next long stop was at Tallahassee," wrote Miller,

where we watered the horses; and we stopped from noon until about five o'clock. Our troop cooked dinner under a tree, and two of the men caught a chicken, and later a man named Stewart caught a rooster. They picked them, and all I saw of the result was some chicken broth for the hospital patients in our car. Troop A caught a small pig, and another Troop had a goose. Then we visited a lot of chicken houses and got ten chickens and two geese. Then we left Tallahassee.

The men must have forgotten that the telegraph had been invented and words traveled faster than trains. Most likely, the mayor of Tampa had received word of the high jinks in Tallahassee, and he was not about to allow the same in the overcrowded streets of Tampa. Since Roosevelt and Colonel Wood were entertained by Governor William Bloxham while the regiment was in Tallahassee, they may not have been fully aware of what had transpired. Either way, the Rough Riders were not warmly received when they arrived in Tampa, and the unit officers, particularly Roosevelt, were offended by the behavior of the civil authorities.

When the final order to move out came to Tampa, the troops were eager to leave their camps and get to the vessels. According to Erna Risch, "Regiments ordered to move early in the evening arrived at the railroad only by daybreak for lack of wagons that never reached them. Despite this disregard for plans, all the troops reached Port Tampa by 11:00 A.M. Some 17,000 troops were moved from Tampa to the port in about 40 hours." The rapid loading of the vessels entailed some major mistakes, such as artillery and other special equipment being loaded on one ship, while the men who fired the guns were on another. Horses were loaded and put into holds with little or no air circulation and few rations of oats and hay. Medical supplies were loaded in the bottom of some holds and were not found in time to treat the wounded once the troops had landed.

These artillerymen oversee the loading of their field cannons on ships prior to boarding the ship themselves. The embarkation of troops bound for Cuba was accomplished rapidly and, if one forgets the carping of Theodore Roosevelt, without difficulties. *Courtesy of the Tampa Bay History Center.*

Loading transports was something new to the American army, which had not left the shores of the United States since the Mexican War in the 1840s. The limited facilities at Tampa greatly hampered efficient organization and loading of transport ships, and the scarcity of trained stevedores, the inexperience of the officers of the Commissary and Quartermaster Departments and the use of cattle boats as transports made loading a tremendous challenge to any force.

Right: Theodore Roosevelt parlayed his adventures as a soldier in the Spanish-American War into a successful career as governor of New York and, later, president of the United States. *Courtesy of the Florida Historical Society.*

Below: Theodore Roosevelt poses with soldiers from the Rough Riders atop San Juan Hill. The capture of this hill was his most memorable exploit as a soldier. *Courtesy of the Tampa Bay History Center.*

When Shafter received the final order to board his men on June 6, 1898, he discovered that only a few ships would be at the docks until early the next morning. The fact that he got the troops, supplies and accoutrements of war loaded and into the harbor in less than forty-eight hours is considered a minor miracle to most military historians. In the larger perspective, the job done by Shafter and the men of Fifth Corps was quite good, even if it did not look so to some of the more notable and literary men on the docks, none of whom had ever been in such a movement before, just like their officers.

14

THE WAR AND ITS
AFTERMATH IN FLORIDA

*The first two decades of the twentieth century were the heyday of railroad
tourism in Florida. Revenues from passengers traveling on the state's
railroads, adjusted for inflation, increased by more than 150 percent from
1901–1915.*
—*William B. Stronge, Florida Atlantic University*

Florida changed as a result of the Spanish-American War. The glaring
problems of easily accessing cities south of Jacksonville, created by the single-
track railroads going into Tampa and Miami, showed the need for an immediate
improvement in the rail lines of the state. Many of the railroad systems in the state
began double tracking their lines and improving their rolling stock. New leaders
moved to the fore of the state's political and economic sectors, and railroads,
which had been the major engines of Florida's economy, were not exempt from
changes in leadership. Henry Plant died in 1899, the year after the war; Henry
Flagler was old and passed from the scene prior to World War I. One by one,
the old owners died off, and soon the lines amalgamated into a few dominant
systems—the Seaboard Air Line, the Atlantic Coast Line and the Louisville
and Nashville systems—all with direct linkages to national systems. Steamship
lines, which were part of these earlier railroad systems, were absorbed into
national corporations or simply went out of business. With the opening of the
Panama Canal, Floridians could take advantage of new opportunities for trade
in the Caribbean, while expanding economies in European countries fueled new
markets for Florida timber products.

The increasing demands for more agricultural products were a boon for
Florida farmers, who were soon growing and shipping tomatoes, potatoes,

limes, lemons, oranges and celery to northern markets. Florida agriculture flourished after the war, particularly when returning soldiers told their friends and families about the exotic fruits and vegetables produced in the Sunshine State. Tourism became the third most important "product" of the state after the war. Hundreds of thousands of dollars poured into the state, and hotels and rooming houses did a brisk business catering to northern visitors.

Everglades drainage projects begun in the 1880s by Hamilton Disston continued farther southward and promised to make cheaper farmland available for settlement. Although today's "environmental historians" cringe at the idea of draining the Everglades, one of the earth's most fragile ecosystems, in the era before the First World War, it was a national headline and drew thousands of new residents to the state. The leaders of that period, like those in Florida today, believed that continuous growth was the way to prosperity. The rapid defeat of the once powerful Spanish Empire gave Americans, especially Floridians, a brash confidence that there was nothing they could not achieve. If we could build a mighty fleet and best the Spanish Empire almost overnight, what else could we do with our wealth and power?

Floridians now felt that they had at least some of the answers.

BIBLIOGRAPHICAL NOTE

The Spanish-American War has garnered a great deal of attention in the last three decades, and we have benefited from the scholarship of many. David Trask's *The War with Spain in 1898* (New York: Macmillan, 1981) is a very good place to start any study of the conflict. Ivan Musicant's *Empire by Default: The Spanish-American War and the Dawn of the American Century* (New York: H. Holt, 1998) is a well-written account of most of the major actions of the war and its impact on America. One of the best studies available, although a bit older, is Graham Cosmas's classic account, *An Army for Empire: The United States Army in the Spanish-American War* (Columbia: University of Missouri Press, 1971). G.J.A. O'Toole's work, *The Spanish War: An American Epic, 1898* (New York: Norton, 1984), is still very useful and very readable. We have noted the works of Erna Risch, Martin Van Greveld, Marvin A. Kreidberg and Merton G. Henry and Richard V.N. Ginn, all official historians with the United States Army or experts in their fields of military history. Their specialized knowledge is invaluable to understanding why this war took place and the problems it created and solved. Our friend and mentor, the late John K. Mahon, worked on his *History of the Militia and National Guard* (New York: MacMillan, 1983) for a number of years, and the results show him as a true master of military history. Ronald Spector's marvelous work, *Professors of War: The Naval War College and the Development of the Naval Profession* (Newport, RI: Naval War College Press, 1977), was very useful in discerning the roles of Luce, Mahan and Soley in forging a modern American navy. Reading Alfred T. Mahan is somewhat of a chore for the modern reader, but the results are worth the effort. The many articles and books written by him or about him show him to be the most important naval theorist of his day. The popular works of Richard Harding Davis, Stephen

Crane and Ralph Paine, although greatly biased, should be consulted. Theodore Roosevelt's works should also be read, but with the caveat that they were self-serving because he was running for political office and thought it politic to make volunteer soldiers seem more important to the war effort than regular soldiers.

Public documents, particularly House of Representatives Document No. 757, 58th Congress, 2nd Session, 1904 (*The Reed Commission Report on Typhoid Fever*) and United States Senate Document No. 221, 56th Congress, 1st Session, 1900 (*The Dodge Commission Report in 8 Volumes*), should be consulted to gain an understanding of what went right and what went wrong with the American military during the war.

For the best look at the role race played in this war, the works of Willard Gatewood should be consulted, especially his book *Smoked Yankees* (Urbana: University of Illinois Press, 1971). More Florida-specific books include Samuel Proctor's *Napoleon Bonaparte Broward: Florida's Fighting Democrat* (Gainesville: University Press of Florida, 1950) and William J. Schellings's dissertation, "The Role of Florida in the Spanish-American War, 1898" (University of Florida, 1958). For a good general background of Florida's economic growth, William Stronge's recently published *The Sunshine Economy: An Economic History of Florida Since the Civil War* (Gainesville: University Press of Florida, 2008) is highly recommended.

Different aspects of the role of Cubans in causing and fighting in this war can be found in Consuelo Stebbins's recent works, especially *City of Intrigue, Nest of Revolution* (Gainesville: University Press of Florida, 2007), and Gary Mormino and George Pozzetta's work, *The Immigrant World of Ybor City* (Gainesville: University Press of Florida, 1998). Armando Mendez's little gem, *Cuidad de Cigars: West Tampa* (Florida Historical Society, 1994), provides a comprehensive look at the cigar industry and the lives of factory workers. Of all the historians who have worked on the Cuban revolutions and migrations, however, the works of Louis A. Perez Jr. cannot be beat for thorough research and readability.

There are numerous dissertations and articles on the role of the press in bringing on the war, a point of view to which we do not wholly ascribe. However, two books, Charles H. Brown's *The Correspondents' War: Journalists in the Spanish-American War* (New York: Scribner, 1967) and, more recently, Joyce Milton's highly entertaining *The Yellow Kids: Foreign Correspondents in the Heyday of Yellow Journalism* (New York: Harper & Row, 1989) are "must reads."

The Spanish-American War was a complex event in American history, and the more one researches, the more information that does not fit into the average textbook version of this war will be found. We hope that this volume will help make more sense out of this important event in America's coming of age.

About the Authors

Dr. Joe Knetsch is a well-respected and highly involved Florida historian. His latest work, *Fear and Anxiety on the Florida Frontier: The Second Seminole War*, was published by the Seminole Wars Foundation in 2008. He is a member of the Florida Historical Society, the Arizona Historical Society and the Southern Historical Society, among others. Dr. Knetsch has written extensively on Florida history, publishing several titles with the Florida Historical Society Press. He is the author of *Florida's Seminole Wars, 1817–1858*.

Dr. Nick Wynne retired in 2008 from his post as executive director of the Florida Historical Society. After obtaining his PhD in history, Dr. Wynne taught college history at several universities, including the University of South Florida. He has published more than twenty books, including several books on Florida history, such as *Tin Can Tourists of Florida, Florida in the Civil War, Florida's Antebellum Homes* and *Golf in Florida*. He is an active lecturer who has given approximately 450 presentations and speeches in the past five years and more than one hundred television and radio interviews. In addition, he has secured more than $8 million in grants during the past twenty years. He is a member of the Southern Historical Association, the American Historical Association, the Florida College Teachers of History, the Georgia Association of Historians and, of course, the Florida Historical Society. He currently resides in Rockledge, Florida (near Cocoa Beach).

Visit us at
www.historypress.net